400

Presented to

_____

by

_____

_____

(date)

LOVING your
Preborn Baby

Carol Van Klompenburg
& Elizabeth Siitari, M.D.

**photos & art
Donalyn Powell**

Harold Shaw Publishers
Wheaton, Illinois

Library of Congress Cataloging-in-Publication Data

Van Klompenburg, Carol.
    Loving your preborn baby / Carol Van Klompenburg & Elizabeth Siitari : photos & art, Donalyn Powell.
        p.   cm.
    ISBN 0-87788-529-X
    1. Parenthood. 2. Pregnant women—Psychology. 3. Fetus—Growth. I. Siitari, Elizabeth. II. Title.
HQ755.8.V35   1990
306.874—dc20   89-70208
                                        CIP

99 98 97 96 95 94 93 92 91 90

10 9 8 7 6 5 4 3 2 1

Contents

Dear Parents,

You've conceived a child? Congratulations! We're happy for you. Pregnancy is a time of joyful anticipation, of looking forward to the birth of your baby. You're planning a new role. But pregnancy itself is also exciting. In these nine months a mother has a physical bond with her baby that will never be repeated. She carries his life within—a life formed from a union of love.

We'd like to help you celebrate that life. We won't teach you how to cope with morning sickness or backache, and we won't prepare you for childbirth or list needed baby clothes. But we will provide you with inspiration and information for celebrating your baby's preborn life. We'll shift the focus of attention from the mother's body to your baby's body and provide a window to her womb, where a marvelous little person is growing and moving and learning.

Twenty years ago experts thought a preborn waited passively for birth in a dark and silent womb. Today we know better: a preborn lives in a sometimes-lit, bustling world, and he responds to it. The womb is a school room, not a waiting room.

We've designed this book for several kinds of reading. You may wish to read it in sequence, beginning with conception (chapter 1) and ending with birth (chapter 13). Or you may use it as a handbook, hunting for facts about your baby at his current age, whether that is six weeks or six months. Finally, you may wish simply to browse, looking at pictures and reading snippets that catch your fancy.

Your baby's age can be counted in two ways: either from the onset of the last menstruation (menstrual age) or from the date of conception (conceptual age). We have chosen to calculate a baby's age from the date of conception. If you and your physician are counting pregnancy weeks from menstruation, you need to subtract two weeks from your baby's menstrual age to find his conceptual age.

One other note: Instead of an impersonal "it," we have chosen to refer to a preborn child as "he" or "she," giving equal time to both sexes. And when we say "baby," we're talking about a *preborn* baby, unless otherwise noted.

Best wishes as you parent your preborn!

Carol Van Klompenburg
Elizabeth Siitari, M.D.

1

You're Having a Baby!

CONCEPTION

When does it begin—
this parenthood?

With the great drama
of hard labor
and first wail?

Or in that magic moment
when sperm
joins egg?

Unmarked,
that microscopic instant
ripples the world,

For life begins,
where it was not

And creates,

still unaware,

a father

and

a mother.

CVK

UNBORN OR PREBORN?

As parents of a preborn, you are not "pre-parents." You are parents! You have already begun to care for your child.

For generations, speakers of English have used the term "unborn baby." Now some are beginning to substitute "preborn baby."

Why the switch? The prefix "un" simply negates the word to which it attaches; "unborn" means "not born." The prefix "pre," however, means "prior to, before."

The difference is subtle. "Unborn" is more negative, calling attention to the child's not being born. "Preborn" points more directly to the baby's current state: she is in the stage prior to birth. Preborn is a more affirming term for your baby. It may stand alone, just like the term "newborn," or—like "newborn"—it may be combined with "baby."

Whether you use unborn or preborn will make a difference in how you feel about your baby. And it also makes a great difference in the way you think of yourself. Often our word choice before birth fails to call attention to our preborn sons and daughters.

When we say a woman is pregnant, we are speaking more about her physical condition than about her carrying a child within—the child is secondary to the condition. Sometimes we say a woman is "expecting a baby" or that she is a "mother-to-be." But she's not expecting a baby—she already has one. And she's already a mother, too.

Each of these terms contains some truth but needs to be balanced with a focus on the baby. One mother says, "I use the term 'pregnant' when I speak of how my life is affected. I use 'with child' when I am thinking more directly of my baby." Perhaps substituting the old-fashioned "with child," or referring to a woman as "carrying a baby," would provide a needed balance in our language.

• • • • • • •

He who sees things from their beginnings will have the finest view of them.

Aristotle

> He [Omoro] said that three groups of people lived in every village. First there were those you could see—walking around, eating, sleeping, and working. Second were the ancestors, whom Grandma Yaisa had now joined.
> "And the third people—who are they?" asked Kunta.
> "The third People," said Omoro, "are those waiting to be born."
>
> Alex Haley
> *Roots*

Life begins for each of us at an unfelt, unknown, and unhonored instant when a minute wriggling sperm plunges headlong into a mature ovum or egg.
Margaret Shea Gilbert

• • • • • • •

A baby is God's opinion that the world should go on.

Carl Sandburg

SECOND BEGINNING

A nurse says,
"Your test is positive,"
Or you see the test tube's color change.

You realize, belatedly,
The miracle within.

You conceive again—
the conception of knowing,
the beginning of love.

This is the dawning
of the feeling of parenthood.

Perhaps it's a bright dawn,
the sun bursting over the horizon
in a blaze of love.

The sun may hurt your eyes.

Or dawn may be
a gradual lightening of the skies
through heavy clouds.

Clear or overcast,
day has begun.

You've changed,
irreversibly.
You are a parent
and you know it.

CVK

*M*others *S*peak
MOMENT OF DISCOVERY

I called the doctor's office from a pay phone for the test results. They were positive! I was so excited I nearly hugged the phone.

> My husband and I did the test together. When we saw it was positive, we didn't say anything; we just hugged each other.

When that little white stick turned a gorgeous blue, Jack went right downstairs and brought out our box of stuffed animals.

> I was so excited. I told two-year-old Sarah, "Your mom's going to have a baby." As soon as my husband got home, Sarah told him. I hadn't even thought she'd remember!

When I walked through the door, Glenn
looked up from the floor where
he was resting, a question mark in his eyes.
I knelt beside him on the soft carpet
and said, "You're a father."
Then I kissed him.

DAWN OF A MIRACLE

We don't have to seek miracles anymore:
The miracle has found *us!*
Carrie Heiman, *The Nine-Month Miracle*

• • • • • • •

For many of us it [pregnancy] is the only time in our lives when we truly stand in awe and are overwhelmed by wonder. . . . It allows us, however briefly, to share in the miracle of creation.

Rachel Smith

• • • • • • •

When a woman decides to bear a child she embarks on the most profound and intimate adventure of which her body is capable.
Gail Brewer and Janice Greene
Right from the Start

Of all possible subjects upon which the artist can draw for inspiration, none has more universal appeal than that of mother and child.
Richard Gelb

LOVE IS . . .

Love is a feeling . . .
. . . melting at your core when you think of the new life within.
. . . tears behind your eyes as you stare at an ultrasound.

. . . an awe-filled "oohh" when you first feel life.
Love is warmth at your center.

Love is a verb . . .
. . . buying a baby crib and diapers.
. . . drinking milk although you hate it—because your baby needs it.
. . . saying no to junk food—because your baby doesn't need it.
Love is acting for your baby's good.

Love is getting to know . . .
. . . reading about your preborn's miniature world.
. . . looking at pictures of preborns your baby's age.
. . . noticing your baby's hiccups and active times.
Love is learning about your baby.

Love is reaching out . . .
. . . talking to your child, when he is still silent.
. . . listening to the quiet voice of her movements.
. . . touching gently, through muffling womb walls.
Love is building bridges toward the person within.

PERFECT LOVE

Love is patient,
love is kind.
It does not envy,
it does not boast, it is not proud.
It is not rude,
it is not self-seeking,
it is not easily angered,
it keeps no record of wrongs.
Love does not delight in evil, but rejoices with the truth.

It always protects,
always trusts,
always hopes,
always perseveres.
Love never fails.
1 Corinthians 13:4-8

For God so loved the world that he gave his one and only Son, that whoever believes in him shall not perish but have eternal life.

John 3:16

Mothers Speak
WHEN LOVE IS NOT THE FEELING

We were not married. When the test tube said "positive" we looked at each other and said, "How will we tell our parents?"

> *I was still a student. When I learned I was pregnant, I was flattened. I wondered if I should just give up and drop out of graduate school.*

When the nurse said I was pregnant, I hung up the telephone and cried. I wasn't ready. The timing was all wrong. I had just signed a teaching contract.

THE WILL TO LOVE

True love is not a feeling by which we are overwhelmed. It is a committed, thoughtful decision.

M. Scott Peck, *The Road Less Traveled*

• • • • • • • •

Sometimes love for a newly conceived child comes in a rush; sometimes it doesn't. Sometimes the child is planned only by God—not her parents. Or sometimes the new life just doesn't penetrate our consciousness. Our child seems ephemeral, more idea than reality. Perhaps first-trimester weariness strips us of warmth, or love ebbs and flows on the waves of nausea.

What do we do when the warm feelings do not grow—or disappear?

When warmth vanishes, we remember that love is more than fuzzy feelings. It is more than jello at our center. Love is the will to reach toward another, to act for our baby's good, sometimes despite our feelings.

Love is an act of will, not a feeling. It may mean hard work. Labors *of* love are easier than labors *to* love. That labor may mean going against the grain of feeling. Maternal labor is not just the grand finale of gestation, but the preceding 9 months as well.

Sometimes when the choice to love is a sheer act of will, the feelings follow. Just as choosing to be gentle and giving with our husbands may re-light romance, so it is with our love for new life.

Occasionally even our will to love fails us. We fail to behave for our child's good. We skip meals, gorge on sweets, neglect our rest. We become self-centered, resenting our discomfort. When we fail, God reassures us of his forgiveness and unfailing love. We have reassurance from his Word: "If we confess our sins, he is faithful and just and will forgive us our sins and purify us from all unrighteousness" (1 John 1:9).

Who Am I?

Am I one
or two
or two-in-one?

Who are we?
Did I conceive a child?
Or, child,
by forming
did you conceive a mother?

Who are we?

I am one.
We are two.

I love you.

CVK

2

Looking Up

Devotions, Prayers, and Dedication

Lord, sometimes
I take control,
playing god.

Within now grows
a child,
unseen,
unheard.

You work your will
molding my baby
beyond my knowing
or control.

Our bodies
follow your plan.

Thank you, Father,
that you are Lord
and we are yours.

Amen.

CVK

HAND MADE BY GOD

Read Psalm 139.

For you created my inmost being;
you knit me together in my mother's womb.
I praise you because I am fearfully and wonderfully made;
your works are wonderful,
I know that full well.
My frame was not hidden from you
when I was made in the secret place.
When I was woven together in the depths of the earth,
your eyes saw my unformed body.
All the days ordained for me
were written in your book
before one of them came to be.
Psalm 139:13-16

What amazing words! God knit me together in my mother's womb, just as he is knitting my baby at this instant. I was not hidden from him, and neither is my child. My days are written in his book of life; so too are my child's.

Thank you, Father, for creating and loving me. Thank you for molding me fearfully and wonderfully from before my birth. Thank you that you love my child already and tenderly watch over him. In your Child's name, amen.

CLOSE TO HIS HEART

Read Isaiah 40:9-11.

> *He tends his flock like a shepherd:*
> *He gathers the lambs in his arms*
> *and carries them close to his heart;*
> *he gently leads those that have young.*
> *Isaiah 40:11*

The Sovereign Lord, the one who rules over all, supreme and mighty, is the same Sovereign Lord who is my shepherd. He gently leads me, his sheep with young. He tends me as part of the flock and loves the lambs—even before their birth.

Jesus, our great shepherd, loved us so much, he gave his life for his sheep and lambs.

Thank you, Great Shepherd for caring for your sheep and lambs, even those not yet born. Thank you for gently leading those who have young. Give me grace to follow your lead. In Jesus' name, amen.

I APPOINTED YOU

Read Jeremiah 1:1-10.

> The word of the LORD came to me, saying,
> "Before I formed you in the womb I knew you,
> before you were born I set you apart;
> I appointed you as a prophet to the nations."
> Jeremiah 1:4-5

Jeremiah was just one of the priests in Benjamin. His beloved nation was captive to a crumbling Assyrian empire. And then the word of the Lord came: Jeremiah was to prophesy. The Lord had known him before conception. The Lord had chosen him before his birth!

Jeremiah, like Moses centuries earlier, protested, "I'm not a speaker. I'm untrained, inexperienced."

But God promised his presence. He had chosen Jeremiah and would give him the gifts he needed.

God promises the same to us: both mother and child.

•   •   •   •   •   •   •

Father, thank you for your promise. I don't always feel equipped to
be a mother. I feel untrained, inexperienced. Thank you for your promise. You have
chosen me and will give me the skills I need. Give me faith in your gifts—and
in your good and perfect gift, Jesus. In his name, amen.

TAKING RISKS

Read Ecclesiastes 11:1-5.

**As you do not know the path of the wind,
or how the body is formed in a mother's womb,
so you cannot understand the work of God,
the Maker of all things.**
Ecclesiastes 11:5

Cast your bread on the waters, says the teacher in Ecclesiastes. When Israelites sent out their ships bearing corn or put out bait for fish, they didn't know the future. They didn't control the rain or the direction the trees fell. They didn't know the path of the wind or how babies were formed.

But the teacher urged them to cast their bread on the water anyway. They couldn't understand—but God did.

Father, I understand only the tiniest fraction of how this child grows within. I don't know the path of the wind. I don't know what the future holds. But I am casting my bread upon the waters with this pregnancy. I am trusting you. In Jesus' name, amen.

A GREATER CALLING

Read Isaiah 49:1-6.

> *Before I was born the LORD called me;*
> *from my birth he has made mention of my name.*
> Isaiah 49:1

"Listen to me, you islands!" shouted Isaiah. "The Lord called me even before I was born, so you must listen. He said I was his servant."

But Isaiah was discouraged. He had prophesied to Israel—calling for repentance and return to the Lord. Israel had ignored him.

Then the Lord who formed him from the womb said, "I will make you a light not only for Israel, but for all the nations."

Father, sometimes I'm tired. You've called me to make a home, and sometimes it turns to chaos. I fail. Or I feel unheard. And then you come again and tell me that I am not only part of a home, but of a larger community. Before I was born, you had a task for me, and you've promised the light that I need. Before my child is born, you know his name. Thank you. In your Son's name, amen.

A CONTINUUM OF LIFE

Read Judges 13:1-24.

> "Now see to it that you drink no wine
> or other fermented drink
> and that you do not eat anything unclean,
> because you will conceive and give birth to a son."
> Judges 13:4-5

An Israelite woman had been sterile, childless. Then one day an angel of the Lord appeared with earthshaking news. She would conceive!

But he had conditions for her pregnancy. Her son was to be a Nazirite, consecrated to God.

Israelites who took the Nazirite vow of separation abstained from wine and other fermented drinks and followed other special rules for the duration of their vows.

The angel told this woman that her son was to be a Nazirite his whole life, not just a fraction of it. And she was to drink no wine.

What's the implication? Samson's Nazirite consecration began even before his birth. His pre-birth and post-birth life were a continuum!

• • • • • • •

Father, thank you for new life within me, which continues on the same line before and after birth. I dedicate this child to your service now, and for the rest of his life. In your Son's name, amen.

A MIRACLE

Read Luke 1:26-38.

> **"I am the Lord's servant," Mary answered.**
> **"May it be to me as you have said."**
> **Luke 1:38**

Mary was troubled. An angel was telling her she would bear a son. "How can this be?" she asked. "I am a virgin."

"With God nothing is impossible," the angel answered. Her cousin Elizabeth, long past menopause, was six months pregnant. The God of this miracle could work another.

Mary bowed her head. "I am the Lord's servant. May it be to me as you have said."

Mary didn't understand—but she accepted. "May it be to me as you have said."

Father, thank you for the miraculous love you showed in sending your Son to be born through Mary.

I understand her confusion, Lord, her disbelief. Sometimes I, too, can hardly believe that I have conceived a child. It seems a miracle.

Thanks for my child—your gift to me.

I am your servant, Lord. In your Son's name, amen.

BLESSED BY FRIENDS

Read Luke 1:46-55.

*My soul glorifies the Lord
and my spirit rejoices in God my Savior
for he has been mindful
of the humble state of his servant.
From now on all generations will call me blessed.*
Luke 1:46-48

Mary hurried to Elizabeth with God's news: Mary would conceive the Messiah.

But God told Elizabeth before Mary did. And as Mary entered Elizabeth's door, the baby John stirred and kicked in his mother's womb.

"Blessed are you!" said Elizabeth. "Blessed are you for believing God's Word."

Mary's mood shifted. She took a step up from simply accepting God's plan. "My soul praises the Lord and my spirit rejoices," she said.

• • •

Lord, thank you for family and friends who rejoice with me in this child. Their joy enriches mine. In Jesus' name, amen.

PERFECT OBEDIENCE

Read Deuteronomy 28:1-6.

All of these blessings will come upon you
and accompany you if you obey the Lord your God:
. . . The fruit of your womb will be blessed.
Deuteronomy 28:2, 4

After fourteen chapters of rules and regulations about idols, unclean animals, feasts, lost property, women captives, tithes, etc., Moses had a promise for Israel: "If you fully obey all the commands I've given you today, you will be blessed in the city and country, when you come in and go out—your calves, lambs, crops—and the fruit of your womb."
"Obey and your children will be blessed," he promised Israel.

Father law-giver, I'm frightened. I don't fully obey you, but I want your blessing for my child. Thank you that Christ obeyed you perfectly, that his obedience covers my sins, and that through him I can claim your blessing on the fruit of my womb. In the name of your obedient Son, amen.

JOSTLING IN THE WOMB

Read Genesis 25:19-26.

**The babies jostled each other within her,
and she said, "Why is this happening to me?"
So she went to inquire of the LORD.
*Genesis 25:22***

• • • • • • • •

Rebekah had been childless, and now God had answered Isaac's prayer. She was with child, in fact, with children! She carried twins.
     She worried. Her children seemed to struggle with each other. She went to an altar and prayed, "Why, Lord, why?"
     He told her she carried two rival nations, and the older would serve the younger.

At birth Jacob emerged second, but he was already tightly grasping Esau's heel. The preborn baby's nature was already inherent and visible. The child was the father of the man.

• • • • • • •

Lord, already my baby's personality is forming. Shape
this little one in your image, and mold him to your service.
In your Son's name, amen.

A GIFT OF GOD

Read Psalm 127.

Sons are a heritage from the Lord,
children a reward from him.
Psalm 127:3

• • •

King Solomon, builder of the temple, reminds the Israelites that unless the Lord builds their houses they labor in vain. Unless he watches the city, they guard it for nothing. And unless he provides fertility, children are not conceived.

God is the sovereign Lord.

He is also generous. He gives houses, protection, and children. "Children are a reward from him."

His people don't need to be anxious, rising early and staying up late. They can find rest because their gracious and giving Lord is in control.

• • •

Gracious Lord, thank you for your gifts, and
for this special gift, a child. Keep me from
being anxious, from thinking I am in charge.
Let me rely on you. In Jesus' name, amen.

IN THE BEGINNING

Read Genesis 1:26-31.

> God blessed them and said to them,
> "Be fruitful and increase in number;
> fill the earth and subdue it."
>
> Genesis 1:28a

On the sixth day of his creative work, God made Adam and Eve. He told them to rule the newly made world.

For that gigantic assignment, they needed help. He instructed them to be fruitful and to increase in number. He told them to conceive and bear children to help them care for his world.

Conception and birth were part of God's world from its beginning, not just for our joy, but for the well-being of all creation.

Creator God, thank you for your vast world surrounding me, and thank you for my role in it. I join an unbroken chain of mothers since Eve who have conceived children to work and worship in your world.

Grant our family a vision of your work for us. In your Son's name, amen.

PRAYER FOR CHILDREN

Father, hear us, we are praying,
Hear the words our hearts are saying,
We are praying for our children.

Keep them from the powers of evil,
From the secret, hidden peril,
Father, hear us for our children.

From the whirlpool that would suck them,
From the treacherous quicksand, pluck them,
Father, hear us for our children . . .

Through life's troubled waters steer them,
Through life's bitter battle cheer them,
Father, Father, be Thou near them.

Read the language of our longing,
Read the wordless pleadings thronging,
Holy Father, for our children.

And wherever they may bide,
Lead them home at eventide.

Amy Carmichael

From *Gold Cord* by Amy Carmichael © 1932 by Dohnavur Fellowship
(Ft. Washington, Penn.: Christian Literature Crusade; London: SPCK).
Used by permission.

PRAYER FOR EXPECTANT PARENTS

Almighty God, your wisdom abounds
in the glory of creation and is beyond
our understanding. Your love for us
and all creatures is as gentle as a
father's and as tender as a mother's.
We give you thanks for creating new
life. Our hearts are filled with joy and
expectation. We proclaim your greatness and ask your sustaining grace for
name(s) of parent(s) that all of us may
grow in wisdom and grace; through
Jesus Christ our Lord.
*Occasional Services: A Companion to
Lutheran Book of Worship*

LITANY OF DEDICATION

Sit side by side at a table, an unlit candle at the center.

Father: In you, Lord, we all have our beginnings.
Mother: In you, Lord, we find the source of life.
Father: Your wisdom is beyond our understanding. Your love for us is gentle as a father's.
Mother: Your love for us is tender as a mother's. And we thank you for creating new life.
Father: We praise your greatness in granting us this, your gift.
Mother: We ask for your sustaining grace in caring for this child, newly begun.
Together: We dedicate this child to you.

(Light Candle of Dedication)

Father: Father, hear us.
Mother: Father, hear us.
Together: We are praying for our child, newly begun, whose life is now part of ours. *(Together place hands over child in the womb. Older siblings may join in this.)*
Mother: Bless this child with your presence.
Father: Enfold him or her in your mercy.
Mother: May he or she be one in whom your glory dwells.
Father: Keep him or her in your love forever.
Mother: Grant us your grace for parenting this child, now and through the hour of birth.
Father: Grant us parenting grace, now and in the years that follow birth.
Mother: We pray for parenthood love, joy, and peace.
Father: We pray for parenthood meekness, mercy, and self control.
Mother: We praise you for this most amazing gift.
Father: In your grace, make us worthy of your trust.
Mother: We praise you, we thank you, we bow in childlike awe before your greatness.
Father: In the name of your Child, conceived in Mary through your spirit, we pray.
Together: Amen.

Keep candle lit through subsequent meal of celebration.

3
Your Growing Child

The history of man for nine months preceding
his birth would, probably, be far more interesting,
and contain events of greater moment, than all the
threescore and ten years that follow it.
Samuel Coleridge

Not all of us will live to be old, but we were each once a fetus. We had some engaging qualities which unfortunately we lost as we grew older. We were supple and physically active. We were not prone to disc lesions and were not obese. Our most depraved vice was thumbsucking, and . . . we ruled our mothers with a serene efficiency which our fathers could not hope to emulate. Our main handicap in the world of adults was that we were small, naked, nameless, and voiceless. But surely if any of us count for anything now, we counted for something before we were born.

Albert W. Liley, Father of fetology

Your hands [Lord] shaped me and made me.
Job 10:8

SILENT MIRACLE

A pin-head-sized egg drifts down a bristle-thick tube, wafted along by tiny waving hairs (cilia) in the walls of the tube. Millions of sperm, hundreds of times smaller than the egg, swim upstream against the current, propelling themselves by whipping their tails. Out of 300 million that entered, only 300-500 have been strong enough to complete their 7-inch journey to the egg. A few make contact, stimulating them to lash their tails even faster as they attempt to penetrate the cell's membrane wall.

Finally, aided by an enzyme it produces to soften the egg membrane, a single sperm penetrates the cell wall, setting up a chain reaction that hardens the membrane against penetration of any other sperm. The sperm continues its wriggling penetration until its head, containing its nucleus with 23 chromosomes, reaches the egg nucleus with another 23 chromosomes.

Over a half-hour period, the nuclei combine. Each provides 23 chromosomes composed of 1 or 2 million genes containing the instructions and blueprints for a unique human being.

Only an hour ago millions of sperm and an egg drifted and swam in the current of maternal fluids; now a being unlike any who has been or ever will be again exists. Boy or girl, brunette or blonde, tall or short, plump or thin, calm or excitable—all traits are mapped out in that pinpoint-sized dot that continues to drift down the 4-inch fallopian tube toward a waiting uterus.

He is microscopic—and complete. All he needs now is nourishment, oxygen, and time. Conception is a moment for bands, angel heralds, and cymbals. A moment for laughter and joy. A moment for thanksgiving and prayer.

But this microscopic cataclysm deep within passes unnoticed by the world outside. Even his father and mother are still unaware that a miracle of life has begun.

WHEN ONE BECOMES TWO

Genetically, hormonally and in all organic respects save for the source of
its nourishment, a fetus and even an embryo is separate from the woman.
Daniel Callahan, Director of the Institute of Society, Ethics and Life Sciences

When sperm and ovum join, there is created at that time a new living being; a being who has never before existed in the history of the world and never again will exist; a being not at the end of the line [like sperm and ovum separately], but at the dawn of existence; a being completely intact and containing within himself or herself the totality of everything that that being will ever be.

Dr. J.C. Willke

•   •   •   •   •

Unless you have an identical twin, there is virtually no chance, in the natural course of things, that there will ever be "another you"—not even if mankind were to persist for billions of years. Indeed, given the vast number of combinations possible among chromosomes, genes, and their smaller subparts, there is virtually no chance that even your own parents could ever come up with another "copy" of you, not even if by some magic they could produce millions of offspring.
Landrum Shettles and David Rorvik
Rites of Life

SCIENCE AND YOUR PREBORN

Medical science uses a range of scientific terms for your baby, such as zygote, embryo, and fetus. Each term refers to a preborn baby at a a different stage of development—although the borders of their meanings are fuzzy. After conception a fertilized egg is called a zygote. (Some scientists use the term *conceptus* instead.) A zygote becomes an embryo. Some definitions say that the embryo stage begins at implantation; others say at 3 weeks. *Embryo* is used to indicate the stage at which body systems are being formed. When body systems are already formed, but simply maturing, the term *fetus* is used for the preborn. Some definitions set this transition at week 5; others at week 8.

Although the boundaries for each of the terms are somewhat arbitrary, the terms are useful for scientists, who need them for detached, analytic work. But parents are not scientific or detached about their child. Such terms stumble awkwardly from their tongues and in their minds can tend to separate the baby's preborn life from her newborn life.

Parents are more comfortable—and rightly so—using the more personal umbrella term "baby."

VITAL STATISTICS

☐ The egg is barely visible to the naked eye, but with a $1/175$th inch diameter, it is one of the largest cells in the body. A light yellow, it is about the size of the period at the end of this sentence and weighs $1/20$th millionth of an ounce. The sperm is much smaller, only $1/500$th of an inch long, a tapering sliver which is mostly tail. It takes 90,000 sperm to equal the weight of 1 egg. However, egg and sperm each contribute $1/2$ of the hereditary material of a baby.

☐ Enough ova (eggs) to produce the world's total population (5.5 billion) would fit in a shoebox. The same number of sperm would fit in a thimble.

☐ The egg is 1 of 2,000,000 that were contained in a mother-to-be already at her own birth. The sperm were produced during the past 60-90 days within the prospective father.

☐ If the strands of DNA codes—which contain the genetic blueprints for life—could be unraveled, the strands for a single adult would stretch several million miles.

☐ Beginning as a single cell, a baby doubles her cells 45 times to form the 30 million which compose an adult. At 7-10 days she has doubled her cells 8 times. By 8 weeks, her cells have doubled 30 times. By birth they have doubled 41 times. The remaining 4 cell doublings are spread over her childhood and adolescence.

ABOUT YOUR BABY'S SEX

At conception a child's sex is determined by which sperm penetrates the egg. All eggs contain only an X chromosome, capable of producing a girl. Some sperm contain an X and some a Y chromosome. If an X sperm penetrates, your baby is a girl. If a Y succeeds, he is a boy.

Around day 56 a baby's sex is apparent. However, without amniocentesis (withdrawal of fluid from your uterus for analysis) or ultrasound, it is impossible to learn your child's sex. His heart rate or position—or any other external indicator—can't tell you. (And even ultrasound specialists have been wrong!)

Long before you know your child's sex, he or she is setting aside cells for producing your grandchildren. At 28 days, when your baby is only 1/8 inch long, his or her yolk sac (a pouch attached to the embryo during early development) produces primordial (primitive) germ cells for future reproduction. These cells later migrate to the site of his testicles or her ovaries.

PREDICTING YOUR BABY'S SEX

There once was a medical doctor who told mothers he could predict a baby's sex by the fourth month. He never told the mothers his prediction; he simply told them he had written it in his big, black book. At birth he would confirm his prediction.

When mothers checked with him after birth, he showed them his book—and they were astounded when his predictions were unfailingly right.

Only at his death was it discovered that he kept two black books.

Superstitions

An old superstition directed parents to hang a pair of pants on the right side of the bed for a boy, on the left for a girl.

Another suggested eating sweet foods to produce a girl, bitter ones for a boy.

*M*others *S*peak
BOY OR GIRL

My mother said I was carrying the baby
higher—that meant a girl. But I also became broad
in back—that means a boy. My husband said,
"See? Twins!"

• • • • • • • • • •

When I was pregnant with our son Nathan, I was sure we'd have a girl, and my husband thought our baby would be a boy. He put his hand on my stomach and said, "Kick 2 times if you're a boy." And Nathan did!

In church Easter Sunday, Lacy, 3, cuddled on my large belly. Our baby felt crowded and gave the 5 hardest kicks of his life. When Lacy learned the baby had been kicking her, she announced she was sure the baby was a boy, because "girls can't kick that hard."

Boy or girl? There can be no choice;
There's something lovely in either voice.
And all that I ask of the Lord to do
Is to see that the mother comes safely through.
And guard the baby and have it well,
With a perfect form and a healthy yell,
And a pair of eyes and a shock of hair.
Then, boy or girl—and its dad won't care.
Edgar Guest

A HOME FOR YOUR BABY

As he journeys toward the uterus, your baby's cells multiply. Thirty hours into his existence, the fertilized egg splits. Then he divides more rapidly, until at 60 hours there are 12-16 cells.

When he enters your uterus about day 3, he is a tight cluster of cells, sort of like a mulberry. He floats in the uterus for 3-5 more days, still dividing, until he becomes a hollow sphere made of 60 or more cells. The rate of his cell division varies, some cells dividing faster than others.

As he journeys and floats, he doesn't really increase in size, just complexity. He simply doesn't have sufficient nutrition—until he finds a home in your uterus when he's around 7 days old and 200 cells large.

He burrows into the soft lining of your tea-cup-sized uterus, spongy and rich in blood. Now he has nutrition, even though the complete process of implanting and taking a firm hold in your uterus will take several weeks. He can begin to grow in size! And he does—at an astounding rate.

The outer layer of his sphere, which will become his umbilical cord and placenta, speeds its growth to support the inner layers slated to form his body. Within that outer shell, he has 3 layers. His outer layer will become his outer skin, hair, sense organs, and nervous system. The middle layer will form his muscle, cartilage, bones, kidneys, heart, and blood. The inner layer will be the lining of his lungs, stomach, bladder, and ear canals. It also will form his liver, pancreas, tonsils, and thyroid.

Your body is not friendly at first. It mounts an immune attack on this invader. Your uterine tissue swells to engulf him. Thousands of your white fighter cells are summoned. But then your body sends messenger cells that attach to your baby's cells. Your white cells recognize the messengers as friends and make peace.

Your body's attack soon turns to welcome. The blood vessels of your uterus become engorged, and the lining glands secrete more fluids for him. He begins to grow.

On a hormonal and chemical level, your interaction has begun!

A NINE-MONTH LIFE SUPPORT SYSTEM

When she nests in the lining of your uterus, your baby begins to form a system for tapping your bloodstream for nutrition and oxygen: a placenta.

Her trophoblast cells (ancestors of her placenta) dig in, interact with your uterine cells, and pass nourishment from the blood to your baby. In succeeding weeks the trophoblast cells become a placenta, a network of blood vessels and membranes that intertwines with your circulatory system, but remains separate.

Nourishment and oxygen can pass across your capillaries (smallest blood vessels) to your baby's placental capillaries. Within an hour or two after you eat, your baby receives nourishment as well. And she can pass carbon dioxide and waste products to you just as efficiently. The placenta also takes over the duty of producing the hormones necessary for your uterus to keep and to nourish your baby.

By 3 weeks her placenta covers 20 percent of your uterine wall. By the time she is 3 months, it covers 50 percent. Fully developed, it is about as large as an 8-inch plate, weighs 1½ pounds, and contains about ½ cup of blood.

At 12 weeks your baby's placenta takes over sending the chemical signal which, among other things, prevents menstruation, thus keeping her nest and nutrition intact along your uterine wall.

At first your baby is surrounded by the placenta, but as she grows, she floats away from the uterine wall, remaining attached to the placenta through an umbilical cord extending from her abdomen. Blood travels through the umbilical cord at 4 miles per hour and completes a round trip through the cord and baby in 30 seconds.

Your baby is surrounded by a membrane sac containing fluid (bag of waters). One-third of this fluid is replaced every hour by your plasma (a clear liquid in your blood).

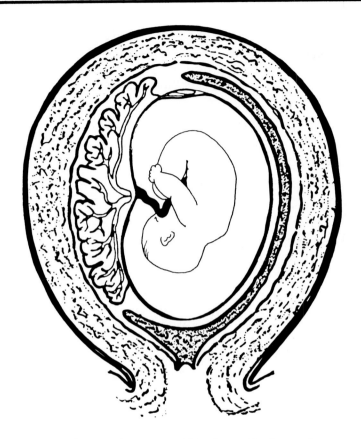

Baby's environment within the mother's womb

A PLAN FOR GROWTH

How is your baby transformed from a ball of cells to a newborn with limbs and organs and face?

Not all at once! At first the cells that split are very similar, but then they start to specialize. He starts out like a one-person workshop, which gradually expands. He adds departments and division heads, dividing and assigning responsibilities to them as he grows. The pattern of development is the same for all babies, although there may be slight variances in exactly which day of his development certain organs or limbs appear.

His growth follows two patterns: His body grows from the top down and from the midline out. Your child's head is first to develop, his brain then able to give orders and receive messages from the rest of his developing body. Head development is followed by the upper trunk and arms, and, finally, the legs and feet.

He also grows from his midline out: His heart and spinal cord develop before his hands and feet.

During the first months of this transformation from single cell, he doesn't look exactly like a newborn. But he looks just right for a weeks-from-conception baby. By 8 weeks, he already looks remarkably similar to a newborn.

CHANGING PROPORTIONS

Because a baby's head develops before his legs, it is proportionately much larger than an adult's. Gradually throughout life, proportionate head size shrinks and leg size increases.

Age	Head (% of body length)	Legs (% of body length)
2 months	50	25
5 months	33	33
Birth	25	40
Adulthood	10	50

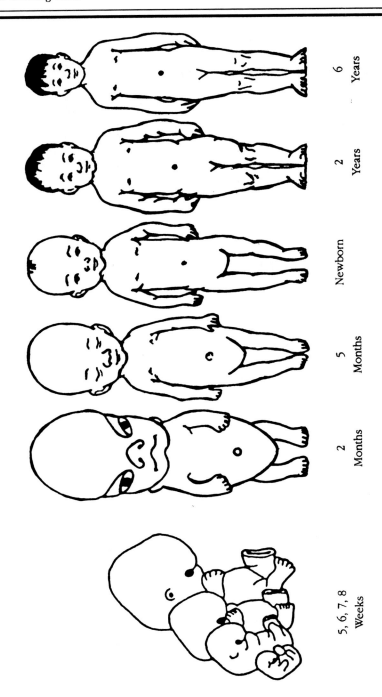

Changes in the relative size of body parts
during embryonic and fetal development for childhood through early adolescence

5, 6, 7, 8
Weeks

2
Months

5
Months

Newborn

2
Years

6
Years

Mothers Speak

VISUALIZING BABY

I pictured my baby like those in
illustrations until he was 8 months along.
Then I began to wonder about his own
special characteristics.

> I followed each month of development. I would
> hold the book pictures up to my stomach, imagining
> what my baby looked like under my skin.

**I looked at pictures—but I
knew our baby had a personality
and was beautiful!**

• • • • • •

*When I tried to picture our baby, I would lie in bed,
studying my husband's features and imagining them
on a baby's soft face.*

FORMING FUNDAMENTALS

MONTH #1

Day*	Development
13	Instead of a sphere, he has become pear-shaped. A bulging streak, to become his spinal cord, appears.

16	A rigid gelatinous rod, his spine, is visible. His body is lengthening, now tube-shaped.
17	Blood cells begin developing.
18	His heart forms. His head begins, as well as his brain and spinal cord.
20	His brain and spinal cord begin to form.
22	A tubular heart is beating. (And your menstruation is 8 days late. You wonder if he exists—and his heart is beating!)
23	Eyes, ears, and nose begin to form.
24	Arm buds appear.
27	Leg buds appear.
28	Blood vessels connect to his heart.
30	3 parts of the brain are present, along with the beginnings of hands and feet, kidneys, liver, and an umbilical cord. His arm buds are tiny rounded knobs. A heart is pumping blood which he made himself.

*The day listed is the typical day for a development. Individual babies may vary slightly from the average day.

By the end of his first month your baby is 10,000 times the size of the fertilized egg. (If this rate of growth continued, he would be the size of planet earth at birth!) He is now ⅕ inch long and could fit easily on your pinky fingernail. His bottom is more like a tail—which will disappear later. His head is ½ of his body length, tucked down and forward.

A single cell has become a body with head, trunk, and the basics of vital organs.

TAKING ON A FAMILIAR LOOK

MONTH #2

Day*	Development
33	Her hands begin to show finger outlines. Her nostrils begin to show elevated rims which are to become her nose and upper jaw. Ear pits appear on the sides of her head.
35	By now, she weighs ¹⁄₁₀₀th of an ounce and is ⅓ inch tall. Her liver begins to produce blood cells.

37 Her arm buds subdivide into shoulders, arms, and hands. The tip of her nose shows in profile. Her eyelids begin as ridges around her eye rims. Her internal hearing organs near completion.

40 Brain waves can be recorded on EEG (electro-encephalogram). Her eyes become pigmented. Her heart begins forming separate chambers.

44 Her mouth palate (roof) forms.

45 Her skeleton is complete in cartilage. All 20 teeth buds are present. Although you can't feel them, she makes her first slight movements (See chapter 4 for more information.)

46 His gonads have differentiated. In her body, 2,000,000 potential ova already exist.

47 Her stomach produces digestive fluids. Her liver and kidneys are operating.

56 Her arms are the size of exclamation marks. She has arms, hands, and fingers; legs, feet and toes—even fingerprints. Her tail has disappeared.

At 2 months, your baby's head has become erect, and her face is recognizably human. She has all the familiar features of an adult: eyes, ears, nose, and limbs. She even has palm creases. But she is less than a thumb's length, about an inch from head to bottom. She would fit neatly in a nutshell. She weighs less than an aspirin tablet (1/30th of an ounce), but she is 50 times heavier than a month ago.

Her head still takes up half of her body size, but that is soon to change.

Development of Human Hands

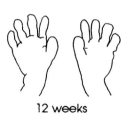

12 weeks

7 weeks

8 weeks

6 weeks

CHANGING PROPORTIONS

MONTH #3

This month, your baby's head growth slows and body growth accelerates. From weeks 7 to 12 body length doubles (from about 1 to 2 inches). Nerve-muscle connections increase, and nerve cells fill a tubular canal where a spinal cord is forming. His kidneys are functioning. (However, at this time they handle only a small fraction of his waste—your blood still filters the bulk of it.)

At the end of this month your baby's eyes are sealed shut. Fingernails and toenails are present, and his or her sex is apparent. (Up to this time sex organs had a similar appearance.) Your baby weighs about 1 ounce and is 2-3½ inches long. He could move around easily inside a goose egg.

Development of Human Feet

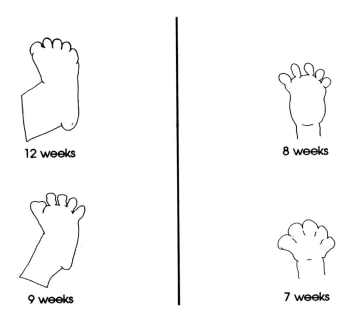

12 weeks

8 weeks

9 weeks

7 weeks

RAPID GROWTH

MONTH #4

During the fourth month, your baby's legs lengthen and the amount of true bone in her body increases rapidly. (Before this time her skeleton was cartilage.) Her vocal cords are complete. She is now capable of crying, but her fluid world prevents her from making sounds. Hair, eyebrows, and eyelashes form. She also has taste buds.

Two temporary features appear: Lanugo (a downy hair which covers her entire body) and vernix caseosa (a greasy, water repellent coating which protects her skin from her salt water environment). Most of the lanugo disappears before birth, but the vernix remains and is washed from her at birth.

Her skin is thin, loose, and wrinkled, lacking a fat layer that will be added the last few months. Transparent, it appears pink or red because of underlying blood vessels.

Her heart is now pumping 25 quarts of blood per day. It can be heard with a special stethoscope, beating 120-160 times per minute, about double your heart rate. Her lungs are formed, except for alveoli (air sacs), which will not be opened until after birth.

At the end of this month she is 6-8 inches long, crown to bottom—about ⅔ of birth length—but she weighs only 6-8 ounces—a small fraction of her birth weight. Growth in length now slows, and she concentrates on weight gain.

Body systems are now in place. The next 5 months are simply a matter of growing bigger and getting ready for survival without her external life-support system.

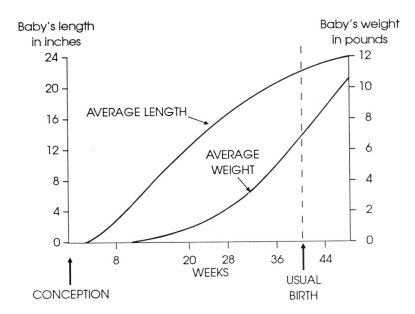

Baby's length in inches

Baby's weight in pounds

AVERAGE LENGTH

AVERAGE WEIGHT

CONCEPTION

WEEKS

USUAL BIRTH

Growth: Growth in length is rapid and consistent until the end of pregnancy. The weight growth is especially rapid during the last two months when most of the fat tissue develops.

PREPARING FOR INDEPENDENT LIFE

MONTHS #5-9

In the 26th week, your baby's eyes unseal. Now he can open and close them. His skeleton continues to harden. At the end of the fifth month he weighs about a pound and is about 12 inches long.

At 6 months he cannot yet regulate his own temperature, but in the coming 3 months he will grow 700 sweat glands per square inch, making temperature control possible. Over the next 3 months, his skin gradually smooths and his body begins to grow plump. Buds for permanent teeth appear behind the milk teeth. He actually has more taste buds now than he will at birth.

During month 7, your baby sheds his lanugo and continues to gain weight. By the end of 7 months, he weighs 2¼-4 pounds and is 16 inches long.

In the eighth month he is likely to settle with his head down, getting ready for birth. Head-down is the most comfortable position in those crowded quarters. By the end of the eighth month, he weighs around 5 pounds and is about 18 inches long.

In the final month, he is in a uterine strait jacket. He does more squirming, less kicking. He has no room for kicking! His heart continues to beat about 120-160 times per minute. Remnants of the lanugo may remain on his face and back. His fingernails and toenails may grow long enough before birth to scratch his face. At birth, 11 percent of his body weight is fat. He is probably 18-22 inches long and weighs 6-10 pounds.

In the 38 weeks since fertilization, your baby has changed from a single cell to an incredibly complex human being. What a marvel!

4

An Underwater Acrobat

ON FEELING MOVEMENT

At 4 1/2 months:
My baby doesn't move around a lot, but I love it when she does. It's the greatest feeling in the world.

At 6 months:
I'm thrilled to have movement inside me so often. My belly bounces sometimes. I wonder if others can see it—and secretly hope so.

At 8 months:
The movement drives me wild with curiosity. I want to know exactly what part that is.

Reminiscing about preborn days:
Nathan was especially active in church—he still is.

For All, a Season

She sits restless
in the lawn chair,
an apple tree behind,
a child within,
impatient for birth.

Seen only through her profile,
he's transformed her walk to waddle
and shortened her breath.

He hears cars pass,
sees the sun's golden glow,
sucks his thumb.

Then, restless, he
stretches,
kicks.

Hand on her belly
she glances down
and smiles.

In due time,
in due time.

For all,
a season.

CVK

DEVELOPING THROUGH MOVING

Until recent years, "quickening" at 16-20 weeks was the only external proof of life within. But ultrasound has opened a window to the womb—and revealed that quickening is not the beginning of your baby's movement at all. She has been moving for some time. Your womb is simply insensitive to any sensation but stretch, and her movements had to be strong enough to be felt by your abdominal wall.

Almost as soon as body structures develop, your baby uses them. Structure and function go hand in hand. Movement is actually necessary for proper development. For example, a baby unable to move is born with severe restrictions of joint movement. Moving her lungs, mouth, head, and limbs contributes to your baby's development.

BREATHING PRACTICE

As early as 11 weeks a preborn baby makes irregular and episodic breathing movements that gradually become more vigorous and rapid. By 16-20 weeks his diaphragm is moving regularly, and in the last 3 months breathing (water, of course, not air) becomes organized and predictable. His voicebox filters hair and bits of skin from the amniotic fluid entering his lungs. Your baby knows how to cry, too, although his fluid environment prevents him from making sounds.

His breathing is affected by the contents in your blood stream, even the amount of time since your last meal. If the amount of oxygen available to him goes down, his breathing slows. It also slows if you take sedatives or drink alcohol.

He may hiccup for as long as half an hour. Some mothers panic when they feel their baby jolting rhythmically 15-30 times per minute, but hiccups are no cause for worry. Their cause is unknown, although doctors speculate they may be tied to babies' drinking of amniotic fluid.

MOUTH IN MOTION

Your baby's mouth opening appears at 5 or 6 weeks. Five weeks later her mouth moves when her face muscles are touched. A baby as young as 9 weeks has been photographed turning her head toward the side of her face that was touched.

At 16 weeks her gag reflex is working. By 20 weeks she can pucker her lips, and 2 weeks later she can suck in surrounding fluid. But fluid isn't all she sucks. As early as 13-18 weeks, she can also suck her thumb, then her fingers, and her toes. Some babies are born with thumbs calloused from frequent sucking.

In her third month your baby begins to perfect some facial expressions by which she will later tell you her moods, likes, and dislikes. And even at this age, individual differences in facial expression are evident. By the fourth month she can frown and grimace. If her eyelids are stroked, she squints.

As early as 10-14 weeks your baby begins swallowing amniotic fluid. However, during months 6-9, babies' drinking habits vary widely. Some daintily sip less than 2 teaspoons of fluid per hour while others guzzle down 16. By 8-9 months, some babies swallow as much as 6 pints of fluid per day.

Their drinking habits before birth correspond to those after. What some babies drink in 2-3 minutes takes others 20 or 30.

ACROBAT PAR EXCELLENCE

As early as 5 weeks (some sources say 6 weeks, others say 8.5), your baby begins moving his arms and legs. He turns, bends his body, head, and back. At first, though, these movements are simply slight, jerky shifts of his body contours.

By 10 or 11 weeks the movements are more pronounced and smoother, like underwater ballet. He uses his arms well, sweeping them around, bending his elbows and wrists. Soon his thumb begins moving in opposition to his forefinger, a preparation for learning to grasp. If his forehead is touched, he turns his head away.

By week 12 he can move his feet and legs, curl and wiggle his toes. He can move his arms, bend his wrists and thumbs, and make a fist. He manages these movements but still weighs less than an ounce. He not only moves—he moves as a reflex response to being touched. His early reflex movements are whole body reactions, a jerking back of his entire body in response to any stimulus. If his amniotic sac is tapped, or his nose is tickled, he moves his arms. By 10 weeks he's sensitive to feather strokes anywhere on his body, except the back of his head.

Gradually his response focuses, narrowing to the area touched. At 4 months, for example, he sucks if his lips are touched; he squints if his eyelids are stroked.

At 9 weeks he grasps an object stroking his palm. By weeks 18-20 his hand touches his face as if exploring it. Eventually he discovers the umbilical cord and explores it when he bumps into it during his gyrations around the amniotic sack.

Your womb doesn't get crowded for him until the final few months. Until then, he makes good use of his space, scooting around like a yo-yo or a jumping bean in a rattle. He's an underwater acrobat. He can do complete flips in 2½ seconds. He is so flexible that he can sit, corkscrew style, with a 180-degree twist in his spine: head facing backward, feet forward. At 26 weeks he can twist his spine and roll over, something he will accomplish after birth only after 4 months of practice. Why? After birth he needs to fight gravity: now he's weightless.

When your baby is 5 months you may be able to recognize a difference between his kicking and turning movements. You may also sometimes guess which body part is pushing your abdominal wall—a foot, elbow, or buttocks.

Also around 5 months, his movements begin to ebb and flow throughout the day. Sometimes he is sleeping, other times alert and active. His sleeping-awake pattern may become predictable, or it may remain erratic.

A Mother Speaks

SLEEPING PATTERNS

They say you can predict your baby's sleep-awake schedule before he or she is born. In fact, every morning as I was reading the script before the show, I would feel the baby wake up—6 A.M. on the dot, the same time every day. While pregnant with my second baby, Lindsay, we wrote down when she seemed to be asleep and awake. She would sleep 4 hours and be up 4 hours. That was what she did after she was born, too.

Joan Lunden
Host of "Good Morning America"

REFLEX REACTIONS AT SEVEN MONTHS

☐ If something is inserted into his mouth, he sucks.

☐ If you touch the side of his cheek, he turns that direction, seeking the source of the touch with his mouth.

☐ At a sudden noise or jolt, he spreads his arms wide, then makes a grabbing, embracing movement. He draws his legs up, and he cries or appears frightened.

☐ If his hand or palm is touched, his fingers and thumb close in a grasping motion.

☐ If his feet touch a surface, he moves his legs in a stepping motion.

GETTING COMFORTABLE

Your baby not only responds to touch but has an apparent pain reaction as early as 16 weeks. She throws out her arms, wiggles her whole body, opens her mouth, and makes silent cries. If a cold solution is injected into her watery world, she kicks violently. She evades needles or microphones inserted into the womb.

She also does what she can to keep herself comfortable. She will turn several times per hour to find a soft spot for dozing. Your backbone is a hard row of rocks to her, and if she ends up with her backbone across yours, she will wiggle and squirm until she is free of that row of rocks.

Perhaps comfort-seeking is the reason twins seem to move more than an average baby. Two of them are seeking comfortable positions in the same space. They rarely choose head-to-head positions—bumping heads is painful! They are like 2 people trying to find comfortable positions in a single bed: they need to adjust to each other's positions.

Comfort also determines the position your baby chooses for birth. Later in pregnancy the uterus becomes shaped like an upside-down pear. Since your baby's head end is smaller than her buttocks when she assumes fetal position, she usually chooses to put her smaller body part in the smaller space and ends up head down.

She chooses a permanent position late in pregnancy, often the eighth or ninth month. Only then does she feel crowded enough to need a permanent position.

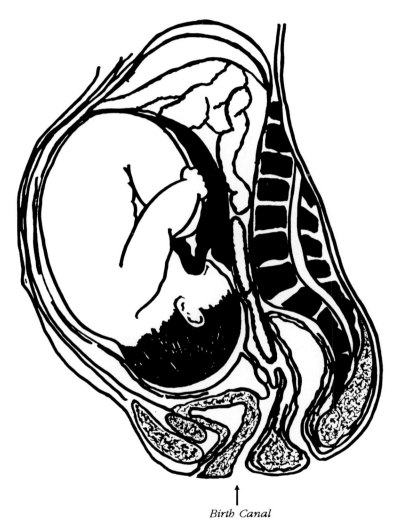

Birth Canal

Position of baby about one month before birth

5
Alive with Stimuli

Sigmund Freud once claimed that a womb was a world "free of stimuli." He was dead wrong. In this world, warm amniotic fluid swirls. Your baby is rocked, squeezed, and shifted as you sit, walk, stretch, and lie down.

His is a world of shifting light, sometimes dark, sometimes lit in twilight-like shadows. Your womb is alive with noise.

Your baby responds to some of these stimuli. Evidence indicates he tastes, sees, and hears.

At birth your baby has months of sensory experience behind him. Your womb is not a waiting room, but a classroom.

A Mother Speaks

When I bend, this child is like a rock inside of me, pushing on the inside—my knees and chest squeezing it from the outside. My flesh and organs take a beating. I'm sure my baby has its own perceptions of the squeeze.

DEVELOPING TASTE

By 14 weeks your preborn's taste buds have begun to form. That same week he begins to swallow. By the third trimester, babies actually have more tastebuds than at birth, and their drinking rates vary widely. Some sip; others guzzle.

Amniotic fluid has a rather chemical taste, like photographic developer—not especially tasty, but not putrid. Your baby's kidneys and sweat glands are functioning in your womb, but the amniotic fluid changes every 3 hours. It is free from the bacteria that cause bad odors and taste in sweat and urine.

Preborn babies respond to changes in the taste of amniotic fluid. In one saccharin experiment, 8 out of 10 babies doubled their drinking rates when the amniotic fluid was injected with saccharin. Their drinking rates crashed immediately upon tasting a bitter, iodine-like substance. Two babies failed to respond to the saccharin. Perhaps they, like some adults, didn't like the taste!

SCENTS BEFORE BIRTH

Soon after birth, babies acquire a keen sense of smell. Before birth, however, babies probably have little sense of smell. Both nostrils are plugged well into the sixth month. Besides, smelling requires air passing the inside lining of the nose.

GETTING READY TO SEE

Two months after conception a baby already has lenses, optic nerves, retinas, and eyelids. Two weeks later, his eyelids fuse shut while the iris and other eye parts develop. By the fifth month his retina (sensory membrane on the back of the eye) can transmit messages, but his eyelids are still shut. In the seventh month the fovea (the tiny spot of clear vision on the retina) forms. Then, between the seventh and eighth months, his eyelids open.

When in this process does your baby begin sensing light? Babies born at 7 months are able to see and to follow moving objects with their eyes.

THROUGH A GLASS DARKLY: WHAT YOUR PREBORN SEES

Does light penetrate your womb? Fetologist Dr. Albert W. Liley says *yes*. The womb, especially one with lots of fluid, may be lit with a strong flashlight in a darkened room. It would be lit even more by sunlight.

Tests show that your baby senses light, even through your abdominal wall and his fused eyelids, as early as 27 weeks. Shine a bright light on your abdomen, and he responds. In 1980 when Israeli doctors flashed bright lights on mothers' abdomens, their babies' heart rates rose by 15 beats per minute. Preborns are sometimes startled by flash photography. Your baby notices changes in light.

The light that penetrates your womb is shifted toward the red end of the spectrum, but is probably too dark for your baby to see any color. His tiny world also lacks interesting visual images.

When born, his vision is 20/500. His world is blurred, except for items 6-12 inches from his face. That's the size of world he's been seeing for the past several months.

A Mother Speaks

I sunbathed when I was pregnant
with Abby. She seemed to sleep then, as if she were
basking in the sun with me.

SURROUNDED BY SOUND

At the University of Southern California researchers inserted a microphone into a mother's uterus so that it rested next to her baby's head. Psychologist Brian Satt remembers, "It was amazing. The first time we listened, we stood around with our mouths hanging open. We couldn't believe it. The clarity was incredible. From people talking 12 feet away to the sound of a cart going down the hall outside the closed door of the lab, the unborn baby heard it all."

A French obstetrician inserted a microphone into a mother's womb just before her baby's birth and tape-recorded these sounds: whooshing noises, the mother's heartbeat, the mother's and doctor's voices, and from a distance, clearly recognizable, Beethoven's Fifth Symphony.

Mothers Speak
MY BABY HEARS

We went to a concert when I was 7 months pregnant. During one song which crashed like an ocean in a typhoon, I thought Ryan would come kicking through his walls.

A door slammed, and my daughter jumped. I knew she could hear! And at 10, she's still the one of our children with the most sensitive hearing.

At college basketball games, our baby seemed to be cheering right along with us. Her activity increased greatly at those noisy games.

When I raised my voice
to my other children
in later pregnancy, my baby moved.
He could hear the difference
in my tone of voice.

•   •   •   •   •

When I was pregnant with Ginger, she jumped in response to hammering and remodeling in the apartment overhead. I knew she heard.

YOUR BABY CAN HEAR

When is a baby capable of hearing sound? By the fourth month her ear is formed, and during the fifth month the bones of the middle ear and cochlea begin to harden. (Hardening is necessary for transmission of sound waves.) By the seventh month, all the structures of hearing are completely formed.

Ultrasound studies show that in that same month babies respond to loud noises by becoming startled and blinking. The earliest response to noise comes at 24 and 25 weeks, and by 28 weeks all normal babies respond to noise.

Other studies document such responses as yawning, making faces, squirming, and heart-rate changes. In one study babies' heart rates rose by 15 beats per minute when music was played. Another study revealed that babies were startled at a loud noise, and then turned in the direction from which the noise came.

Might these babies be responding to a chemical signal from their mothers instead of to the sound? Researchers checked by preventing mothers from hearing the sounds and by using deaf mothers. The babies responded anyway.

The evidence is conclusive. By 28 weeks, preborn babies hear.

YOUR NOISY INTERIOR

What does your baby hear in her watery world? She hears the world of your interior! When you walk, the noise of your vibrating bones makes your womb noisy. Your swallowing and intestinal gurgles also reach her. (If you drink ginger ale, the bursting bubbles sound like Fourth of July fireworks inside of you.)

The continuing and comforting lub-dub of your heart and arteries provides a steady rhythm for your baby. And your voice, traveling through your bones and body tissue is a familiar sound to her.

From the outside, voices like her father's are softer than yours. Responses to microwave beeps, dryer buzzes, and telephones have been recorded.

Not only do preborn babies hear, but they distinguish differences in sounds. When researchers played classical music a bit louder than normal, babies' heart rates increased. But their heart rates did not increase in response to the same note played over and over. Play Vivaldi, they relax. Play Beethoven, they kick and move.

Several researchers have found that preborns move in rhythm—to their mother's voice, the beat of an orchestra drum, the pulsing of a single melody line.

Researchers disagree on the volume needed for a sound to be heard. Some say the sound needs to be fairly loud—110 decibels or so. Others say the preborn can hear sounds of 72-84 decibels. (Zero is no sound, 65 is just audible, and 130 is the pain level.)

Regardless of the volume needed, mothers and researchers agree: Your baby hears, as well as sees. That's exciting to know as you answer your doorbell, turn on the stereo, and talk on the telephone. Your baby is aware!

HEARING AS YOUR BABY DOES

Because your baby is surrounded by water instead of air, the sounds that reach him have a different quality from those that are airborne.

What does your interior sound like? Try walking on a hard floor while plugging your ears with your fingers. The low-pitched, echo effect you hear is similar to the sound of your interior.

Your husband can hear how your voice sounds to your baby by resting one ear on your abdomen, plugging the other, and listening to the vocal tones that reach him through your body tissue.

6

Your Baby's Learning Process

When music director Boris Brott conducted, he occasionally experienced a strong sense of déjà vu. Rehearsing a string quartet, he knew what the music would sound like before he turned the page—and the cello part was especially clear. The same phenomenon occurred with other music. He was mystified.

He mentioned the mystery to his mother, a professional cellist. He recalls, "I thought she'd be intrigued because it was always the cello line that was so distinct in my mind. She was; but when she heard what the pieces were, the mystery quickly solved itself. All the scores I knew sight unseen were ones she had played while she was pregnant with me." Brott was a musical prodigy, and few adults recall music heard before birth. So you need not immediately sign up for cello lessons to provide a proper musical environment for your baby.

But research, still in its infancy, is beginning to verify that fundamental learning begins even before birth.

*M*others *S*peak
ON SHARING MUSIC

I know my baby hears. So I try to listen to music every day, and every Saturday I listen to the classical radio station. Music is very important to my husband and me, and we want to share that with our baby.

• • • • •

We played soothing music
after a busy day.
It probably helped me, too.

WHEN CONSCIOUSNESS BEGINS

When does a baby become aware? Experts are not sure.

To be aware—to process information—your baby needs at least 3 developed structures: neocortex (a specialized section of the brain), thalamus (a gland at the brain center), and neurons (the fundamental cells for nerves to transmit messages). By 6 months a preborn has all 3 structures in place, and consciousness is possible.

Dr. Dominick Purpura, editor of *Brain Research* and a medical school professor, believes awareness starts between 28 and 32 weeks (in the sixth month). At this point, he says, the neural circuits are just as advanced as at birth, and the brain is mature enough to support consciousness.

Research on pre-birth learning supports his opinion.

FUNDAMENTAL LEARNING

When South African researchers vibrated mothers' abdomens during the last 10 days of pregnancy, their babies' heart rates and movements changed. The babies responded to the vibration. However, when the researchers repeatedly used the vibration, the babies' response steadily declined—they became accustomed to it.

Other research repeats these results: present third-trimester babies with a noise and their pulses race, or they are startled. Keep repeating the noise and their response subsides.

Mothers have reported the same phenomenon. When the radio first blares, their babies may kick in protest. But the kicking soon diminishes.

What's happening? Babies are learning! They are becoming accustomed to a noise or vibration (habituation) and they no longer respond.

Preborns also learn to associate two events. A Cornell research team first gently vibrated mothers' abdomens. Their babies did nothing. Then researchers slammed together 2 pieces of wood. The babies were startled. The research team then combined the two events: the clapper and 5 seconds of vibrating, followed by 4 minutes of rest time. After 16 clapper-and-vibration episodes, most babies jumped when just the vibrator was used. They had learned to associate the two events. Their response had become conditioned.

Both habituation and conditioned responses require remembering. In the last 3 months babies begin fundamental learning!

QUIETED BY YOUR HEARTBEAT

The lub-dub of your heart dominates your baby's world of sound before birth. It provides a rhythmic, dependable core. And, after birth, babies seem to be comforted by heartbeat sounds.

When psychologist Lee Salk played a continuous, tape-recorded heartbeat for newborns in a New York hospital nursery in 1972, he found that they gained more weight and cried less than babies who did not listen to heartbeat sounds.

Other studies have duplicated his results. In 1976 Dr. Murooka, an obstetrician at the University of Tokyo, played a heartbeat for newborns and found that they quieted and fell asleep soon after they heard it.

Anthony DeCasper found that newborns prefer the sound of a recorded heartbeat to a man's voice.

What are the implications? Babies are comforted by a familiar sound—one that they apparently remember from the womb.

CHOOSING MOTHER'S VOICE

Upon learning that preborns can hear their mothers speaking, psychologist Anthony DeCasper wondered if they had learned to recognize their mothers' voices.

He decided to check the babies' preferences. But how could they indicate that preference? DeCasper devised a pacifier by which newborn babies could choose the tape recording piped into their headset. By changing their sucking pattern, they could choose which tape they heard.

He gave them a choice of their mothers' voices reading *To Think That I Saw It on Mulberry Street* and another woman's voice reading the same story.

Eighty percent of the newborns chose their mothers' voices.

Whether they were bottle-fed or breast-fed, separated from mom at birth or with her continuously made no difference. Already 48 hours after birth their preference for mom's voice was consistent.

A French experiment verified his findings. Researchers videotaped newborns' responses to taped recordings of their mothers' voices and other women's voices. Analysis of the videotapes revealed that they responded more frequently to Mom's voice.

Before birth your baby begins to remember—and like—the sound of your voice.

RESPONDING TO DAD'S VOICE

When Anthony DeCasper checked babies' preferences for their fathers' voices, he found that they had no preference. Even after a father had spent 1-4 hours speaking with his child after birth, the baby still did not consistently choose the tape recording of his father's voice over another man's. Thus, Casper concluded, a baby's preference for mom's voice is something he acquires before birth.

Dr. Thomas Verny, however, in *The Secret Life of the Unborn Child*, says that a newborn—even in the first hour or two after birth—does prefer his father's voice if, before birth, the father has consistently spoken to the baby in short, soothing words. Given opportunity, babies learn to know their fathers' voices as well as their mothers'.

A Mother Speaks
RECOGNIZING DAD'S VOICE

Every night my husband, Michael, would talk to my tummy. He'd say, "Hello there, this is your father speaking," and then he'd sing a musical scale. He always did the same thing. When my first baby, Jamie, was born, she cried endlessly. Then Michael held her. He said, "Hello, this is your father speaking." And he sang the scale. The baby looked up at him and stopped crying.

Joan Lunden, Host of "Good Morning, America"

REMEMBERING STORIES AND MUSIC

After Anthony DeCasper documented that newborns recognize their mothers' voices, he tried a new experiment. He asked mothers of preborns 7½ months along to read a story aloud 3 times daily for 4 weeks. Then he monitored the babies' heart rates as their mothers read the familiar story and then an unfamiliar one. Babies' heart rates decreased during the familiar story and increased during the unfamiliar one. Even before birth, their response to the two stories differed.

DeCasper also tested newborn preferences. He asked 12 mothers to read stories aloud 2 times per day during the last 6 weeks of pregnancy. Half read *The Cat in the Hat* and half *The King, the Mice and the Cheese*. He let newborns choose which tape-recorded story they would hear their mother reading (using the same pacifier-controlled tape recorders as in earlier experiments). The newborns chose the story they had heard before birth.

Researchers at Queens University in Belfast, Northern Ireland, discovered that newborns respond to music they've heard before birth. Psychologist Peter Hepper observed 15 newborns during a soap opera episode on Irish television. Seven of the mothers had watched the program every weekday while pregnant. The others had not.

When the theme music came on, the babies whose mothers had watched the show became attentive. Hepper said, "If they were crying or making a noise, they immediately stopped and became alert as if they were watching the show. But the children of the non-watchers simply carried on what they were doing."

Whether it's stories or music, newborns respond to sounds they have heard repeatedly before birth.

A WORD OF CAUTION

One enthusiastic mother, upon learning that preborns could hear and remember, walked into a local bookstore and requested a book to help her teach the alphabet to her preborn baby.

Entrepreneurs have noticed the research and developed products to fit it. One claims that babies can be taught the alphabet and also science and social studies before birth through mental telepathy. Another has planned a program for teaching your baby a fundamental vocabulary (pat, rub, mom, dad . . .) before birth. A prega-phone (megaphone attached to a cord to aid in speaking with a preborn baby) has been created.

Experts advise caution for parents hoping to produce superbabies by prenatal learning. Regarding his discovery of memory of prenatal sounds, Anthony DeCasper cautions, "This doesn't mean that the baby understood. It doesn't mean that the baby can learn ABCs or that it learned to understand what the cat [in the hat] did." Researchers have not yet discovered just what newborns recalled: repetition of the word "cat," the pattern of different words, rhythm, the tempo, or some other element.

Michael Meyerhoff, Associate Director of the Center for Parent Education in Newton, Massachusetts, advises, "To say that a fetus understands words, remembers words, and makes decisions *in utero* is ludicrous. Typical first-time parents can be misled."

About prega-phones, Dr. Thomas Verny says, "I certainly don't see anything wrong with it, but the prega-phone doesn't work any better than speaking normally."

Your child is probably not learning alphabet letters or calculus, but something more fundamental—and far more important—the rhythms and tones of speech and music, and the sound of your loving voice.

7

Love Is a Potpourri

Who am I, Lord?
Just yesterday I was
an hourglass
(roughly, anyway).

Now I balloon
forward
outward
(even backward, I fear).

I resent
(sometimes)
my loss
through this gain.

What am I saying?

My ballooning
creates a safe haven
for a little one
you already love.

Give me x-ray vision, Lord.
Keep in my sight
your child,
my child.

Let my outline fade
as I focus on
our child
within.

Amen.

P.S.
Please let the hourglass
replace the balloon
in your good time.

CVK

THE BEST OF TIMES, THE WORST OF TIMES

A baby is an inestimable blessing and bother.
Mark Twain

Warm love for your preborn baby may not be possible every moment. You can't order love instantly from a fast-food menu of feelings. It may compete with other wide swings in your emotions.

For both physical and emotional reasons, mood swings are as much a part of pregnancy as weight gain. When you conceive, the progesterone level in your blood stream rises. (It's the same hormone that increases prior to menstruation, except that during pregnancy it reaches even higher levels.) This progesterone level prevents menstruation and maintains your pregnancy. But for many women it also produces moodiness. You may feel dull and sluggish.

Even without the hormone shifts, the momentous role transition of pregnancy produces stress. On a life-stress scale of 100, pregnancy rates a stress value of 40. (Death of a spouse rates 100 and being fired from a job rates 47.)

All the changes—physical and emotional—can produce wild mood swings set off by a mild event. The official word for these swings is *labile*, which means "readily undergoing change, unstable."

When you're feeling unstable, remember that the moodiness is normal; it's a healthy sign.

M. Scott Peck's words about growth are true also of the growth into motherhood: "Move out or grow in any dimension, and pain as well as joy will be your reward. A full life will be full of pain. But the only alternative is not to live fully or not to live at all."

ABOUT PREGNANCY'S MOOD SWINGS . . .

The Anglo Saxons made allowances for pregnancy's mood swings—huge allowances. Under Old English law a pregnant woman's testimony was not accepted in court because she was considered unreliable.

She smiles, she weeps, she feels ravenous or bilious,
she wants company, she wants solitude—all in the course of the
same day, and quite possibly even before lunchtime.
Peter Moyle
How to Be a Pregnant Father

*M*others *S*peak
ABOUT MOODINESS

The Monday after Mother's Day I couldn't stop crying. I resented my husband and felt overwhelmed by everything because I was pregnant. My changing body, thinking about day care and feedings, getting up at night with my baby, diapers . . . This mini-hysteria lasted a day. Now I just experience brief periods of feeling overwhelmed.

> Today life seems hard. I wish it were summer and I were twelve years old again, lying on a hill by myself. Why is it necessary to grow up and become serious about everything? Will there ever be another carefree day?
> **Sarah O'Connor**
> *The Nine-Month Journey*

I have sometimes experienced depression and lack of hope, which have at their root the failure to assent to life, its trials as well as its joys. I said, "Yes, I want to be part of life" but affirmation is not a one-time matter. That yes, which is actually a yes to God and what he intends for me, must be repeated continuously.

Sarah O'Connor
The Nine-Month Journey

Emotions throughout Pregnancy

Three months dreary,
three months cheery,
three months weary.
Old Proverb about pregnancy

For many women pregnancy has 3 emotional stages. In the first 3 months (trimester) your life is dominated by fatigue, nausea, and a dreamlike sense of unreality. The second trimester is a honeymoon period, when fatigue and morning sickness fade; you thrill to feel life, and labor is in the distant future. The final few months are often filled with impatience. Pre-pregnant days feel like ancient history, and you are eager for delivery.

During the 9 months, many women also experience shifts in their ties with their baby. At first you begin to accept pregnancy as fact, but you think of your child simply as part of yourself. Later (often when you feel life) you become aware of your baby as a separate human being. This awareness is the foundation for a relationship, for a mother's bonding with her child.

*M*others *S*peak
STAGES OF PREGNANCY

HARDLY REAL . . .
The reality really didn't hit me for awhile. It was like having a prolonged case of the flu.

I just felt bloated and premenstrual with weariness sighing through my veins. I didn't feel like a mother at all.

REALITY DAWNS . . .
Suddenly now at 6 months, I finally feel truly pregnant.

I can be thinking about politics or the weather or what to have for dinner when the realization suddenly strikes me anew that I, Sarah O'Connor, am pregnant. I will have a baby. This is happening to me.

Sarah O'Connor
The Nine-Month Journey

BABY BECOMES IMPORTANT . . .
I spoke to a friend about feeling obsessed with the thought of a baby coming. She said my attitude was natural.
Sarah O'Connor
The Nine-Month Journey

The baby makes me feel responsible and serious and sometimes a little lonely. I feel so close to this little person that I can't yet see. And that gets in the way of closeness with other people.

NINTH-MONTH IMPATIENCE

One day Mildred wrote to a friend:
"Today all I did was sew on a button."
Helen Good Brenneman
Meditations for the Expectant Mother

• • • • • • • •

> **The only time a woman wishes she were a year older is when she is expecting a baby.**
> **Mary Marsh**
> **quoted in *Stork Realities***

• • • • • • • •

If pregnancy were a book,
they would cut the last two chapters.
Nora Ephron
Heartburn

• • • • • • • •

I hope the end is soon. Heartburn, diarrhea, swelling. . . . I am ready for my old body back again. . . . It's time for the baby to find a place of its own. . . . I need a little room.

Sarah O'Connor
The Nine-Month Journey

"Wait for the LORD;
be strong and take heart
and wait for the LORD."   Psalm 27:14

IRRITATING INCONVENIENCES

Of course, everybody knows
that the greatest thing about Motherhood
is the "sacrifices," but it's quite a shock
to find they begin so far ahead of time.
Anita Loos

At times your baby seems to be running the show. She is. And losing control of the show may trigger resentment in you. Your waistline disappears as your middle swells. You feel tired. You give up foods you like, or eat foods you don't care for. Your interest in sex may waver, and you may feel clumsy during intercourse. In fact, you may feel clumsy around the clock. You may feel that friends notice your pregnancy more than they notice you.

You may feel guilty because of your resentment, telling yourself that you have no right to be irritated. Such guilt is unwarranted. Fleeting resentment of these changes is as normal as excitement and enjoyment in the adjustment time of pregnancy.

ON CHANGING SHAPE

I was square and looked like a refrigerator approaching.

Jean Kerr (expecting twins)

Like a kangaroo wearing earth shoes.
Erma Bombeck

*M*others *S*peak
FLEETING RESENTMENT

On changing shape . . .

I'd always been trim and never thought much about it. When I grew bulky and heavy, I suddenly realized how important looking slim had been to me.

The flip side . . .

Some women complain that they can no longer
see their feet. I'd just as soon not.
They're nothing great to behold anyway.

I like looking in a mirror when I'm pregnant. The more I show,
the more I love it.

On pregnancy requirements . . .

I hate to watch what I eat, get more sleep, give up jogging, and watch my body turn to jello.

My husband wouldn't let me have caffeine, and I went through chocolate withdrawal. Also, I was sick the first 4 months. I sometimes thought, "Hey this is enough!" But then I'd realize a baby was worth the sacrifice.

The resentful feelings come and go
and are due to vanity. I always think of this baby
as God's gift, but sometimes I wish he could happen
without some of the changes
my body has to tolerate.

> *I had not wanted another child (this was number 4). I don't think it was bad to feel resentment, fear, exhaustion—it was reality. I did not want another baby—in the abstract. But somehow that wasn't how I felt personally toward this particular baby.*

A WRINKLED BROW

I've spoken with hundreds of pregnant women.
I've yet to meet the one who considers herself
the Perfect Pregnant Woman.
Most harbor secret fears of not measuring up.
Ellen Sue Stern
Expecting Change

Causes for anxiety abound during pregnancy. You may worry about approaching labor and delivery, about your baby's health and normalcy, and about your parenting abilities. You may even worry—with a hint of excitement—about the possibility of twins. Sometimes, in panic, you wish you could turn back time to a pre-pregnant day and rethink your decision. You're uncertain of your ability to cope with parenting. But you can't turn back. Your baby *is,* and with his life something sacred has begun.

It's comforting to know that such anxieties are common. Most mothers of preborns experience some of these worries. It's also comforting to know that, most of the time, fears are unfounded. The overwhelming odds are that you will have a normal, healthy baby. And the chances of twins are only 1 in 88. Chances of triplets are only 1 in 7500.

*M*others *S*peak
ANXIETY ATTACKS

I taught Sunday school while I was pregnant,
and a student with Down's Syndrome consistently
sought me out. I worried that it was
God's way of preparing me.

• • •

Last night I looked down at my stomach and panicked. It was like the first time I looked down from the top of a ski lift and realized I couldn't return the way I had come. My only way out was to ski down that mountain criss by cross. There was no way out of this pregnancy either. This morning it was better, though. I've decided that I will make it down the mountain, criss by cross, no matter how long it takes.

• • •

*A friend began describing her labor, delivery,
and stitches in graphic detail. I panicked, closed my eyes,
and asked her to stop. I couldn't handle it.
I was too frightened.*

• • •

I hated the thought of the impending birth—
there was no turning back. It scared me.
Sometimes I wished I weren't pregnant at all.
I've met other moms who felt the same way.

FEAR OF LOSS

Having conceived a child, many parents fear losing her. They hear of miscarriages, premature births, and worry about the survival of their child within. Such fear is normal. We're afraid to lose those we love. That fear is especially strong among parents who have already lost babies through death.

But sometimes that fear inhibits love. We're afraid to grow attached because loving leaves us open to pain. One mother, pregnant again after losing two children, said, "As desperately as I wanted my baby, I was terrified at how vulnerable I was making myself."

In her book *Free to Grieve,* Maureen Rank, who has lost several preborn children, says:

> As my age and number of pregnancy losses increased, so did the fears that gripped me. Like many women, I found myself holding back from anticipation of the baby growing inside, playing a little don't-get-involved-and-you-won't-get-hurt game in case we didn't make it to term again. . . . And I purposely left the baby things in storage and the nursery dismantled almost until the very end, not wanting to chance a disappointment.

However, Maureen advises against following her example. "All my paltry self-protective devices did not protect me from fears about the pregnancy outcome. Those insidious what-ifs edged in anyway. Thinking negatively did not make fears go away; it only drove away my joy."

Fight the urge to play it safe. Love your preborn baby, despite any risk of pain or loss.

*M*others *S*peak
FEAR OF LOSS

Some women at work
had miscarried. I was afraid of getting too
attached to my baby, just in case
that would happen to me.

● ● ● ● ● ● ●

After losing two premature babies, I was afraid to get too attached to Jenny. I was afraid of losing her.

> I would dream I miscarried, wake up, see my tummy, hug the baby and say, "Thank you, God." I don't take a preborn day or month for granted.

I loved my baby all I could
during pregnancy because I felt that might be
my only chance.

*"Do not let your hearts be troubled.
Trust in God; trust also in me."*
John 14:1

**I sought the LORD, and he answered me;
he delivered me from all my fears.
Psalm 34:4**

The Lord is near. Do not be anxious about anything, but in everything by prayer and petition, with thanksgiving, present your requests to God. And the peace of God, which transcends all understanding, will guard your hearts and your minds in Christ Jesus.

Philippians 4:5-7

Mothers Speak

BUT THE GREATEST OF THESE IS LOVE

In spite of my fears and worries, I can't think of a more glorious and miraculous privilege than to carry a life inside of me. Sometimes I marvel that I get to do this—am doing it this minute!

I was mildly complaining about being
pregnant. My husband said, "It's wonderful. Just think of it!
Reproducing yourself—creating new life!"
He loves this baby.

I miss my daily 2-mile run, but I walk to compensate. I get tired of the come-and-go hunger. Yet, often I enjoy being pregnant, knowing I care for a special little being with the incredible closeness only a mother can experience.

8
Good Health for You and Your Baby

Self discipline is usually love, translated into action.
M. Scott Peck
The Road Less Traveled

BASIC HEALTH RULES FOR MOTHERS OF PREBORNS

1. Consult your family physician early in your pregnancy (by the second month), keep your appointments with him or her, and follow his or her advice.
2. Get enough rest.
3. Get a moderate amount of exercise.
4. Eat a balanced diet.
5. Avoid alcohol and caffeine.
6. Don't smoke.
7. Don't take over-the-counter drugs without consulting your physician.

RECOGNIZE WARNING SIGNS

Contact your physician immediately if:

1. You experience bright bleeding from your vagina.
2. You faint or have a severe headache.
3. You have blurred vision, or see spots or flashes of light.
4. Your face or hands become swollen or puffy, and you suddenly gain weight.
5. You have chills or fever.
6. You experience a sudden gush of fluid from your vagina before 8½ months of pregnancy.
7. Your baby does not move for a 12-hour period, or moves less than 10 times in a 24-hour period.
8. You have abdominal pain.
9. You vomit persistently.
10. You experience pain when urinating.

EAT WELL—FOR YOUR BABY'S SAKE

Good nutrition is essential for a healthy pregnancy. It's an important investment in your baby's well being. And care for her well-being is a dimension of love.

Ideally, nutritional deficiencies and dietary problems should be resolved even before conception. Your diet influences the egg's development even before ovulation. It affects the number and the quality of eggs produced.

The essential nutrients of growth (amino acids, vitamins, protein) play an important role in the fertilized egg's first cleavage (splitting into 2 cells) and subsequent division into organ systems. These nutrients may play a role in the ultimate size of your baby.

Good food is important for you and your baby. You need to eat well to help with the birthing process, to keep you healthy, to build a healthy baby, and to prepare yourself for nursing, should you choose this method of feeding.

Pregnancy is NOT a time to diet! The American College of Obstetrics and Gynecology recommends a weight gain of 22-29 pounds during the average pregnancy. Even an overweight mother should gain 12-18 pounds.

A Mother Speaks
ON MORNING SICKNESS

We had tried unsuccessfully for 5 years to have a child. So I was convinced that my round-the-clock nausea was a flu. When the lab technicians came back smiling and gave us the results of a pregnancy test— POSITIVE—I said, "But when you are pregnant you have MORNING sickness, not all day and all night."

One of the technicians, who was also pregnant, answered, "Believe me—you can be sick almost any time it's inconvenient."

Mothers Speak
ON WEIGHT GAIN

> The most useless piece of advice I got during pregnancy
> was: don't gain too much weight—but (drink) 4 glasses of
> milk, (and eat) 4 pieces of bread, 8 ounces of protein,
> potatoes, fruits, vegetables, 2 eggs, prunes, bran, and
> some butter and oil every day.
>
> Joan Gore
> quoted in *Stork Realities*

I was *always* hungry. Apparently I ate
too much junk food because I gained 50 pounds.
It was a good lesson—I'll never
eat that way again.

YOUR WEIGHT GAIN: WHERE DOES IT GO?

Although the 22-29 pound weight gain is for the baby's well-being, the baby
is only 7½–8½ pounds of your gain. The remaining pounds help provide for
your baby. Where do they go?

- ☐ 1½ to 2½ pounds to your placenta, amniotic fluid, uterine tissue growth
- ☐ 4 to 5 pounds to increased blood cells
- ☐ 4 to 5 pounds to increased body fluids,
- ☐ 1 pound to breast enlargement
- ☐ 4 to 5 pounds to body-fat stores and protein

NUTRITIONAL ADVICE

Teenagers and women weighing less than 100 pounds before pregnancy have special nutritional needs. They should have nutritional counseling from their doctor or from a dietitian where they receive medical care. So should mothers with multiple babies, gestational diabetes, heart, or kidney problems.

Ideally, every pregnant woman should have a nutritional dietary assessment during her pregnancy. Many health plans and insurance companies already allow for this. Nearly all hospitals and larger clinics have nutritionists and registered dietitians to help you. Take time to check out your diet.

Mothers Speak
ON NUTRITIONAL ADVICE

With my fifth pregnancy I learned that I had gestational diabetes. The nutritionist was wonderful! Menu planning became easy and fun. I felt better than I had with my first four pregnancies.

I consulted a dietitian during my
third pregnancy. She was very helpful. I felt awful
until I began to eat in a more balanced way. She helped me
determine my needs and plan
how to meet them.

THE NUTRITIONAL NEEDS OF A GROWING BABY

Your preborn baby's nutritional needs require that your diet increase in protein, calcium, iron, minerals, and vitamins:

> *Protein.* Your preborn needs about 80 grams per day for developing his brain, muscles, skin, and nervous system. Protein is especially important in the last half of your pregnancy.

> *Calcium.* Your need for calcium increases by about 1200-1500 mg. per day, for your baby's bone development. If her increased dietary needs for calcium are not met, your baby will borrow calcium from you, which can lead to bone loss and increased risks of osteoporosis later in life. The last half of pregnancy is again the most critical, when your baby starts to build strong bones.

> *Iron.* Approximately 60 mg. per day are needed for red blood cell development. Your baby will take approximately 300-500 mg. of iron from you during pregnancy.

Vitamin and Mineral Supplementation. Controversy exists as to the exact needs and allowances for some minerals. We do know that .8-1.0 mg of folic acid is needed for brain growth and nervous system development. Twenty milligrams per day of zinc are required for many chemical interactions during growth. Vitamin B 12 is especially important for vegetarian mothers.

It is important to remember, however, that vitamin and mineral supplements should never be a substitute for good nutrition. Large doses of vitamins and minerals are not necessary—and may actually be harmful.

Calories. The actual increase in need for calories during pregnancy is not excessive. The average mother needs only 300-400 calories per day over the 2100 calorie baseline normally required. Your protein, calcium, fat, vitamin, and mineral needs, however, are substantially changed. Therefore, it is important to eat nutritious foods. In other words: MAKE EACH CALORIE COUNT!

RECOMMENDED DAILY DIETARY ALLOWANCES FOR PREGNANCY

Energy (Kcal)	2,400
Protein (gm)	78
Vitamin A (IU)	5,000
Vitamin D (IU)	400
Vitamin E (IU)	15
Vitamin C (mg)[1]	80
Folic acid (mg)	.8
Niacin (mg)	16

Riboflavin (mg)	1.7
Thiamin (mg)	1.4
Vitamin B6 (mg)	2.5
Vitamin B12 (mg)	.004
Calcium (mg)	1,200
Phosphorus (mg)	1,200
Iodine (mg)	.175
Iron (mg)	30[2]
Magnesium (mg)	450
Zinc (mg)	20

[1]All units from here to the end of the page are listed in milligrams. Some vitamin lists use the microgram measurement. A thousand micrograms equal 1 milligram.

[2]If bodily iron stores are normal.

WHAT TO EAT AND HOW MUCH

Four food groups should be included when you plan your daily menu: meats, milk and dairy products, fruits and vegetables, and breads and cereals. The foods below are not a comprehensive list, but only a guide to help you start.

MEATS

You should have 4-6 servings of meat per day.

Meat	Serving Size	Calories	Protein (grams)
Bacon	2 strips	100*	4
Beef	3 oz.	245	15
Cheese (American)	1 slice	105	6
Chicken	3 oz.	100	17
Egg	1 large	80	6
Fish sticks	4 (4 oz.)	170	17
Lamb Chop	3 oz. (broiled)	300	15
Ham		245	21

Hot dogs	2 medium	350*	14
Peanut Butter	2 tbsp.	170*	8
Pork Chop	3 oz.	320	14
Shrimp	3 oz.	100	16
Tuna	3 oz. (in water)	110	18
Turkey	3 oz.	160	20

*High fat.

MILK AND DAIRY PRODUCTS

You should eat 4-5 servings of milk and dairy products per day.

Food	Serving Size	Calories
Buttermilk	1 cup	100
Cottage cheese	1¾ c.	355
Hard cheeses	1½ oz.	140
Ice cream	1 cup	235*
Milk (skim)	1 cup	90
Milk (2%)	1 cup	140
Milk (whole)	1 cup	160*
Milk (malted)	1 cup	500*
Yogurt (plain)	6 oz.	110
Yogurt (fruited)	6 oz.	180

*High fat.

FRUITS AND VEGETABLES

Use fresh fruits and vegetables as much as possible. They are higher in nutrients and fiber and lower in calories, sugar, and sodium than canned or frozen. You should have 4 servings per day.

Fruit	Serving Size	Calories
Apple	1	70
Banana	1	80

Cantaloupe*	½	80
Grapefruit*	½	60
Grapes	25	90
Orange	1	70
Orange juice*	½ cup	60
Peach	1	35
Pear	1	100
Pineapple	1 cup	80
Raisins	¼ cup	105
Strawberries*	1 cup	55

*Good source of Vitamin C.

Vegetable	Serving Size	Calories
Asparagus	½ cup	20
Beets	½ cup, cooked	30
Broccoli	¾ cup	30
Corn	½ cup	70
Green beans	½ cup	20
Lettuce	¼ head	20
Peas	½ cup	60
Potato	1 med. baked	90
Spinach	½ cup	20
Squash	1 cup	30
Tomatoes	1 small	30

BREADS AND CEREALS

Try to include whole and enriched grains and high-fiber foods in your 4 servings per day.

Food	Serving Size	Calories
Bagel	1 small	160
Cereals (non-sugared)	¾ cup	60-105

Dinner roll	1 medium	100
English muffin	1 (half)	150
Graham cracker	1 square	30
Oatmeal	½ cup	65
Pancakes	1 4-inch	60
Rice	½ cup, cooked	90
Saltine cracker	1 square	20
Spaghetti noodles	¾ cup	140
Sweet roll	1 medium	130-180
Waffle	1 4x5-inch	210
Whole wheat bread	1 slice	65

SAMPLE DAILY MENU

This menu provides you with ample calories, protein, and Vitamin C for a day.

Breakfast
Orange juice, 4 ounces
Milk, 1 cup
1 egg, poached
Whole wheat flakes, 1 cup

Snack
Yogurt with fruit

Lunch
Turkey sandwich (2 slices whole wheat bread
with 2½ ounces shredded turkey and
1 teaspoon margarine and 1 tablespoon
 mayonnaise.
Peach
Milk, 1 cup skim
Cole slaw

Snack
Granola bar
Apple

___

Dinner
Roast beef, 2-3 slices
Boiled potatoes
Sweet potato
Pudding, 1 cup

___

Bedtime
Dried apricots
String cheese

ABOUT BEVERAGES: CAUTION!

For baby's sake, whenever you dine,
Try to avoid both coffee and wine.

Why should you avoid coffee when you're carrying a preborn? Because, in animal studies, excess caffeine has been linked to birth defects. No safe limit has been set for caffeine in a pregnant woman's diet. The U.S. Food and Drug Administration recommends that pregnant women avoid or decrease their caffeine intake. Beverages containing caffeine include coffee, hot cocoa, tea, and many soft drinks (e.g. *Pepsi, Coke, RC Cola, Mountain Dew)*. Foods containing chocolate and over-the-counter drugs such as *Dristan* and *Anacin* also contain caffeine.

Drinking alcohol during pregnancy is also unwise. Not only does alcohol have a negative effect on the growing baby, but it is heavily laden with calories that provide little nutritional benefit. It's an unwise addition to your menu.

A few quick reminders:
1. Limit the use of artificial sweeteners.
2. Take a daily vitamin and mineral supplement.
3. Select foods high in calcium, vitamin C, and iron daily.

*M*others *S*peak
ON SELF-DISCIPLINE

Now and then I felt deprived when I wanted pop with caffeine—but I had no problem saying "no" to them.

> I *love* chocolate, but I gave it up during my pregnancy. My baby is worth the sacrifice.

I love to eat junk food and drink wine on holidays. It was hard to give up some of those little things.

I realized that the baby was part of me and that by taking care of myself, I was taking care of my baby's needs.

WHAT YOU DRINK, YOUR BABY DRINKS

Folklore that the placenta screens out harmful substances is not true. Within minutes of your drinking alcohol, it enters your bloodstream. Once there, it immediately crosses the placenta and enters your baby's bloodstream, where it depresses her central nervous system.

In London, doctors watched the breathing of 6 preborns before and after their mothers drank a glass of orange juice. The babies "breathed" 46 percent of the time. But after moms drank orange juice mixed with a bit of vodka, they breathed only 14 percent of the time.

Although alcohol begins to affect your baby about the same time it affects you, it remains in her bloodstream longer than yours. In addition to entering through your placenta, alcohol also enters the amniotic fluid surrounding your baby. It is removed from the fluid only half as fast as from your bloodstream. As your baby swallows amniotic fluid, she remains intoxicated long after you have recovered.

Alcohol has poisonous effects on preborns both directly and indirectly. The direct by-products of alcohol metabolism (especially acetaldehyde) are particularly toxic to a developing baby because her central nervous system is very susceptible to these by-products. Indirectly, alcohol injures the placenta and causes malnutrition. The placenta seems to be harmed in its ability to transfer nutrients to the baby.

HARMFUL EFFECTS OF ALCOHOL

Throughout history people have suspected a relationship between alcohol and birth defects. In 1968, Dr. Lemoine pioneered the study of alcohol-related birth defects. His work was followed by reports of a grouping of fetal malformations which eventually was termed Fetal Alcohol Syndrome. This syndrome includes small birth size (especially a baby's head) and a face with narrow eyes, a low nasal bridge, and a short, upturned nose. Half of these babies have heart defects. Some researchers believe that Fetal Alcohol Syndrome now outranks Down's Syndrome and spina bifida (defects in spinal development) and is now the leading cause of mental retardation.

The most consistent abnormality for babies of heavy drinkers is retarded growth. This defect in growth is never made up by the baby after birth, since his cell size and numbers of cells have been permanently damaged.

Studies have also shown decreases in brain-cell numbers and size along with decreases in the chemicals that are needed to transport information from one area of the brain to another (neurotransmitters). Damage to fine motor and gross motor skills at 7 years of age has been documented in children whose mothers drank heavily. Of these children 30 percent had I.Q.'s of less than 80 (100 is normal) compared to 9 percent of children whose mothers who did not drink.

Problems with nearly every organ system in the developing baby have been observed in mothers who drink heavily. There is a 38-69 percent increase in major and minor abnormalities among children of drinkers. Language disabilities, sleeping problems, and skeletal malformations have been recorded.

There appears to be an increase in first- and second-trimester bleeding, infection, and tearing loose of the placenta, as well as in miscarriages and stillbirths in women who drink.

Women who drink excessively may also smoke, take other drugs, and have poorer nutrition. Therefore alcohol-related birth defects may have multiple causes (so it's difficult to pin the blame on alcohol usage alone).

The safe limits of alcohol consumption are difficult to define since every individual varies in his or her susceptibility to damage. How much is too much? Most research has been done with alcoholic patients. Alcohol intake has varied from 1.5-4 drinks per day. Effects on the baby also vary with the age at which the baby is exposed, the mom's blood alcohol level, and the length of use of alcohol during pregnancy.

But the risk is clear. The safest choice is to drink no alcohol at any time during pregnancy.

SMOKING AND PREBORNS

When a woman smokes, she inhales as much carbon monoxide as if she were puffing on the exhaust pipe of a car. Cigarette smoke contains many other poisons and drugs such as nicotine and cyanide. Nicotine readily crosses the placenta. It causes an increased heart rate and respiratory rate in the baby. Carbon monoxide binds to hemoglobin much more easily than oxygen does. This dramatically decreases the oxygen supply to the baby and can produce oxygen starvation. Oxygen is needed for all growing cells—a lack of it can lead to small babies. The average birth weight for children of heavy smokers is ½ pound less than for children of non-smokers.

Smoking not only lowers babies' birth weights, but it increases both their rate of childhood respiratory disease and their death rate before and after birth. Studies of mothers who smoked 1 or more packs per day showed a 20-35 percent increase in fetal death rate.

Why is there an increased death rate with smoking? The placenta has problems more frequently; it may come loose or bleed. The membranes of the amniotic sac may rupture easily, leading to infection and early birth. Studies indicate that smoking mothers may also have a higher rate of miscarriage.

Babies of smokers have been shown to have lower scores at both 1 and 5 minutes after birth on the Apgar test (a scale for rating infant health).

After birth, nicotine in breast milk causes babies to be irritable, having increased heart rates and diarrhea. It can also decrease the breast milk supply.

The American Academy of Pediatrics Committee on Environmental Hazards states: "The message is clear. For the health of our children (at least), please don't smoke."

A CAUTION FOR SMOKING FATHERS

A father's smoking may affect the health of his preborn child. When doctors at Case Western Reserve Medical school measured the amount of thiocyanate in babies' umbilical cord blood after birth, they found more of it in the cords of babies whose mothers smoked. (The body produces thiocyanate when exposed to cyanide, a poisonous by-product of cigarette smoking.)

Thiocyanate level was also significantly higher for babies whose fathers smoked.

FOR THE ROAD AHEAD

You will only have your child as a preborn for 9 months. Following the good nutrition guidelines we have talked about in this chapter will help to make those months—and your baby—healthy and happy. And it will be good for your body, too.

9
Bonding with Your Preborn

When Karen found out she was pregnant, she stopped at a store on the way home to buy a sleeper for her new baby.

Marie and Jack cleaned out Jack's den and started making it into a nursery the day after Marie's pregnancy was confirmed.

Rachel and her husband started talking about their baby every day as soon as her pregnancy test was positive. "He became part of our daily lives, and I wasn't even showing yet," says Rachel.

Parents use different channels, but they express their feelings for their baby in tangible ways as soon as that baby becomes real in their hearts and minds. For some that is earlier, for some later in the pregnancy.

In her study of preborns as members of families, Colleen Stainton remarks, "It is quickly apparent that parents do form a relationship with their unborn baby during pregnancy and construct for themselves, as a couple, a perception of the infant as a separate other."

Some experts feel that parental attitude is important to the well-being of preborns. In *Rites of Life,* Shettles and Rorvik say, "Studies indicate that women who bond with babies still in the womb (as well as immediately after birth) generally have offspring who are mentally and physically healthier throughout their lifetimes. . . . You will not be wasting your time and effort if you try to communicate your love and acceptance of your baby well before it is born."

THE MIRACLE OF MOVEMENT

For many parents, the first sensations of their babies' movements are a turning point.

Those first sensations are fluttering, uncertain. In *Of Woman Born,* Adriene Rich says, "In early pregnancy, the stirrings of the fetus felt like ghostly tremors of my own body." Some women are unsure whether they're feeling the baby move, or internal gas.

Some women say it feels like bubbles bursting, or like butterflies. Some say it feels like a tiny finger poking you inside. One mom who loves to read thinks it feels like the pages of a book blowing in the wind inside of her.

Your baby has already been moving 11-12 weeks before you feel those first tentative flutters at 16-20 weeks. But in that moment your baby may become for you, for the first time, a person separate from you. Now bonding can begin.

For some moms, feeling movement of unplanned infants brings acceptance of new life. Other mothers begin preparing, making purchases. They have images of what the baby is like and will be like. They feel more attached to that little person inside.

*M*others *S*peak

FEELING LIFE

**The first time I knew it was the baby kicking,
I thought,
"There are two of us in this office now."**

Neither of my pregnancies seemed real to me until I felt movement. It was a relief. I had no other symptoms and deep down I wondered, "Is there really a baby growing inside of me?"

*I hadn't wanted this pregnancy. I was still in school.
So I didn't let myself think about the baby. Then one day,
when I was climbing the stairs, she turned and kicked
around inside me. I sat down at the top of the stairs and
cried. I hadn't been thinking about her. After that I made
time to sit and think about her each day.*

RESPONDING TO MOVEMENT

As your baby grows, her movement within becomes a way of life for you and you respond to that movement. Some mothers believe that rubbing and massaging their abdomen is comforting and soothing for their babies. Some play games with the protruding part; others try to guess which body part is causing the visible lump.

With your physician's help, you may be able to make some accurate guesses about your baby's position in the final months of pregnancy. The picture of your child within may become clearer.

Mothers Speak
RESPONDING TO MOVEMENT

I played a little game with our baby when his hand or foot protruded. I'd gently tap it, and he'd move it to a new spot. So I would nudge him again.

• • •

I really couldn't imagine what our baby looked like until I saw pictures. As I felt movement, though, I started picturing her legs, arms, and head, and I imagined which of her body parts was poking me.

• • •

It's fun trying to figure out if it's a knee
or a foot she's talking to me with.

It's so hard to guess the parts. I think I'm only good enough to distinguish a main body part from an appendage. The rump feels like the head and an elbow feels like a knee. My baby is usually in breach position, so I took the doctor's word for what was at which end.

Sometime later, I felt massive movement and could tell he'd switched poles. I'd just love to have a transparent abdomen to really see what's going on in there.

I like to rub my stomach and convey by touch the love I already have for her.

When I was pregnant with Abby, my sister died. At the funeral home, where pain hung in the air so I could hardly breathe, Megan sat on my lap. "Mommy," she said, with a 3-year-old's attempt at a whisper, "the baby just kicked me."

At that moment, I loved that preborn child fiercely. I knew that child would help us all—in her very newness, in her innocent and gentle arrival in the middle of all our hurt, guilt, and confusion.

THE THRILL OF HEARING AND SEEING: DOPPLERS AND ULTRASOUNDS

For some mothers, a physical bond with their baby may precede feeling life. They may hear his heartbeat on a doppler, or see her on an ultrasound screen.

A Doppler or Doptone registers the sound of a preborn's heartbeat and magnifies it. It can pick up the heartbeat of a baby 7-12 weeks from conception. By sending intermittent high-frequency sound waves into your uterus, an ultrasound produces a picture of a preborn on a television-like screen. It is most often used between the twelfth and twenty-fourth weeks to determine the age of a baby.

Many ultrasound technicians provide a black-and-white photo of the preborn baby for parents to keep. Some parents have even brought videotapes with them and taken home a movie of their baby.

For some women the deep realization of their baby as a separate person occurs when viewing an ultrasound picture. In *Rites of Life,* Landrum Shettles and David Rorvik say, "When women are shown ultrasound images of their unborn babies, they very often experience what has been called the 'shock of recognition,' recognition that what they are seeing is human life and that it belongs to them. They identify or 'bond' with the unborn baby after seeing even a fuzzy picture of it in the womb."

After studying mother-infant bonding during ultrasound, Dr. Larry Platt said, "Early bonding helps to put into parents' minds the fact that the fetus is a patient and that they the parents must take care of themselves better."

After viewing ultrasound, one mother who had been considering an abortion said, "I feel that it is human. It belongs to me. I am going all the way with this baby."

*M*others *S*peak
HEARING HEARTBEATS

What an incredible thump and whoosh it is!
Phyllis Chesler, *With Child*

• • • • •

To me, my baby was no longer just a concept.
I really was pregnant. That day seems more like the beginning
of my pregnancy than conception.

• • • • •

There came a point when I doubted. Were the test results accurate? The first confirmation—hearing the baby's heartbeat—was such a thrill!

Mothers Speak
SEEING ULTRASOUND

I fell in love with my baby when I saw it.

• • •

It was indescribable. I couldn't take my eyes off the screen. I was almost 8 months along, and seeing our baby for the first time gave me an even more special sense of closeness and bonding. I was struck with awe. I felt like crying and laughing and screaming with excitement all at the same time. My only regret is that my husband was not there with me.

> What really created a picture of my baby was viewing the ultrasound. That established for us the human life that was inside of me. The baby was so active during the second ultrasound that it brought his realness to our attention.

I could hardly believe how God was knitting that little being together.

We have an ultrasound photo with the others in the album. It's labelled "Casey's First Photo."

Ultrasound photo caption: "Still Life of an Approaching World."
Phyllis Chesler
With Child

TALKING WITH BABY

With the current evidence that babies hear voices—and even remember them—some parents are spending time talking with their preborn children.

After studying 25 couples, Colleen Stainton concluded that mothers talked with their preborn babies—especially when alone with them. She observed, "Seven mothers volunteered that they talked to the fetus when in the bathtub or while dressing. . . . Three mothers reported they chatted with their fetus in the car en route to and from work. Five mothers described their talking as 'inner talk' where thoughts and feelings were communicated to the fetus without words. Most of these parents felt their fetus listened to them in a state of quiet alertness."

Talking strengthens your bond with your preborn!

*M*others *S*peak
TALKING WITH MY BABY

Last night I felt wide awake. So I sat for awhile talking to the baby, telling him how glad I was he was there and for the first time telling him I loved him.

> *I often apologized for yelling or ranting. I wanted the baby to hear gentle voices— enough harsh sounds were coming.*

**I would sing to my baby and caress her.
I felt this was soothing to her.**

My favorite time to talk to my baby was in a nice warm bath. I would lie back and relax with my hands on my stomach. I talked about the day's activities or the baby herself.

•   •   •   •   •   •

When I read to my older girls,
I always felt I was
reading to the baby, too.

•   •   •   •   •   •

I talked to her about everything. My husband Mike did, too, but said it was hard to hold a conversation with my belly! She seemed to know our voices right away when she was born.

•   •   •   •   •   •

We talked to our baby throughout pregnancy, introduced ourselves, told him how much he was loved, what we were doing. I read the Bible aloud during the day, and my husband read it aloud at bedtime.

*M*others *S*peak
PRAYING FOR MY BABY

I pray for my preborn baby by name every day.

At night when I check on each of my children, I put my hand on their foreheads and pray Aaron's benediction, "The Lord bless you and keep you; the Lord turn his face toward you and give you peace" (Numbers 6:24-26).

Now I do it for our baby, too.

I sometimes pray, "Father, thank you for this child. We know so little about her, but we ask that she may be exactly as you've chosen her to be. Equip her with the talents you've chosen her to have for you. Make your claim on her and never let her wander from your path. In your Son's name, amen."

During pregnancy, I relied on God much more than usual. I realized that even if I did everything right, life was still in his hands. I hadn't felt that helpless before.

KEEPING A JOURNAL

Martha kept a diary through each of her 4 pregnancies. When Agnes, her firstborn, turned 18, Martha presented her with excerpts from the diary of her preborn days. Martha wanted to provide her with a sense of her beginnings, her roots. Now Martha's other 3 children are asking when they will receive their diary copies.

When we asked mothers to write answers to our questions about their preborn babies, they responded with enthusiasm, investing many hours in creating a record of their pregnancy events. When they finished, many said that answering our questions had been good for them. It had given them a chance to reflect on and record a unique span of their lives. Some kept photocopies of their answers.

Some mothers use journal writing to work through their mixed feelings about their new babies. Some use the time for looking back, for collecting information about the family tree and photographs of ancestors.

Others record important world news items as well. Some include pregnancy photos (they don't feel photogenic, but they realize that a decade later they'll enjoy the record).

You may wish to create a written record of your pregnancy and your preborn's life. Writing will strengthen your bond—and provide a memento to be treasured.

CREATING A JOURNAL

Questions to Consider

☐ When did you suspect you were pregnant?
☐ How was your suspicion confirmed? How did you feel? What did you think?
☐ How did you tell your husband? Describe the event.
☐ How did you find a name for your baby? When did you decide on the name(s)?

☐ How are you feeling? Do you feel tension between your needs and those of the baby? How do you resolve that tension?

☐ Describe sharing the news with other family members and friends.

☐ Describe hearing your baby's heartbeat and/or viewing her ultrasound.

☐ What are your causes for concern and worry?

☐ What are your sources of joy and anticipation?

☐ Write any Scripture passages that are especially meaningful to you at this time.

☐ Describe the first time you felt life.

☐ Describe the first time your husband felt your baby move.

☐ Do you talk to your baby? Describe some of your conversations.

☐ Do you pray for your baby? Write a prayer for your baby.

☐ If you have older children, describe any ways in which they have become involved in your preborn's life.

☐ When did labor begin? Describe your labor and your baby's birth, birth weight, length, time, etc.

Other Items You Could Add to Your Journal

☐ Letters to your baby at various stages of your pregnancy

☐ Pictures of yourself at several stages of pregnancy

☐ Records of your weight, doctor appointments, physical symptoms, your first day in maternity clothes

☐ Clippings of top news stories from the 9 months of your pregnancy

☐ Family tree or information about ancestors

10

Loving: A Family Affair

When my Baby Stirred . . .

I woke up last night when my baby stirred within me.

With awe, I lay motionless, wondering.

Then a gentle wave rippled across me again.

I laid my hand gently on my tummy and felt the flesh move under my fingers like a very quiet, full swell on a summer lake. The kind that gently rocks an anchored boat because the waters were disturbed by a motor boat that passed far off.

Somehow at that moment my baby became real to me.

With my other hand I reached across and ran my fingers through my husband's hair.

"Huhhh?"

"Want to feel something?" I guided his hand to where mine was resting. We lay in the dark, not talking, waiting. After what seemed like a long while there was that same faint ripple, then a sudden movement up that collided with my husband's hand.

He chuckled.

"He'll make a good football player," he said contentedly and rolled over and went back to sleep.

Mildred Tengboom
Devotions for a New Mother

A FATHER'S LOVE

Rodney Clapp discovered his fatherly feelings in a moment of panic. A few weeks after learning his wife was pregnant he came into the bedroom late one night to find her sitting upright, rigid with pain.

He described his reaction in *Christianity Today*: "I asked her what was wrong, and before she could answer I had crossed the room and was sitting next to her, pressing urgently on her abdomen. 'It's my allergies,' she said. 'My throat is burning up.'

"It was hard not to display my relief. Sandy was no less distressed, but the baby was in no danger, and that had been my immediate, visceral fear."

Looking back, he was intrigued by the intensity of his protective feelings. His child was just a few weeks along, and already he experienced a father's love.

The need for fatherly love has not always been acknowledged—even after birth. John Bowlby, for example, wrote in 1951 that a father "is of no direct importance to the young child, but is of indirect value as an economic support and in his emotional support of the mother." The stereotype of a father helplessly wringing his hands in a waiting room while his wife labors in the delivery room has spilled over onto both sides of birth.

But Rodney Clapp is not alone in his protective love. Many fathers show active care and concern for their preborn children. Psychologist Dr. Kay Standly, who studied pregnancy at the National Institute of Health, concluded that most husbands are truly interested in their preborns and in their wives' pregnancies. In fact, Dr. Stanley concludes, apparent lack of support and involvement may often be simply a mask for anxiety.

Childbearing in the Sixteenth Century

Several centuries ago, even male doctors were excluded from birth. It was the province of midwives. In 1522 a male physician disguised himself as a midwife to watch a birth. When his deception was discovered, he was burned at the stake.

*M*others *S*peak
YOU'RE A FATHER!

When I found out I was pregnant,
I came home and said to Larry,
"Hi Dad." He cried.

•   •   •   •   •

I bought a card, inserted a baby bib and the test results and laid the envelope just outside the shower. When he stepped out and found it, he was very excited.

•   •   •   •   •

My husband did the pregnancy test for me, and then telephoned me and said, "Hi, Mom. No more coffee!"

•   •   •   •   •

It was as if we had our very own secret for awhile, and we wanted to talk and giggle about it together.

•   •   •   •   •

**My husband said, "I think of you
in a different light now that you are
carrying our baby."**

Born Loser

my wife upstairs
sewing a new
maternity dress

me down here
in the basement
writing my poem

a competition
of creativity

the winner
decided perhaps
by the fact that
in my first draft
of this poem

what was then
the second stanza
is now the first

Hugh Cook

Reprinted by permission of the author

FATHERHOOD

Fatherhood, like motherhood, produces a mix of feelings. Fathers may be unsure about their parenting skills. They may wonder about the time demands of children or worry about the added finances required.

Amid this confusion about the future, their wives begin to make new emotional and physical demands. They also change in disposition and shape.

In *How to Be a Pregnant Father,* Peter Moyle describes the father's feelings: "For the first-time father, pregnancy can be puzzling, tiring and sometimes hurtful, a frequent strain on the patience and the digestion."

"We expect a good deal from expectant fathers," he says. "They are from the beginning supposed to be happy, sympathetic, understanding and available. They are expected to cater to their partner's needs and whims, and to accept and adjust to any alterations in their normal give-and-take pattern without difficulty or complaint."

Husbands may be pleased by the new demands, or they may feel low, burdened, and left out.

One father, despite a tight budget, kept buying very expensive stuffed toys for his preborn baby. When he brought home a 5-foot, musical teddy bear, his wife became angry. He was hurt. "You know, it's my baby, too." he said. His wife got the message. He was feeling left out.

One mother shared, "My husband told me that he was a little jealous that I could experience the pregnancy and he couldn't. Of course, as the months went by, and he saw how uncomfortable I was, some of the envy wore off!"

Despite their mixed feelings, though, fathers find ways to express their love for their preborn babies. They feel their movement, talk with them, and pray for them. Some fathers enjoy learning about fetal development, going along on medical check-ups, hearing the baby's heartbeat, or seeing an ultrasound. Viewing an ultrasound often brings the father into the pregnancy too. He often gets more excited about the picture than the mother does.

A father can find creative ways to express his protective love and share the joy of his child's preborn days.

*M*others *S*peak
SHARING MY BABY'S MOVEMENT

It was very exciting when my husband could feel movement. We shared a bond with the baby that way. With the first pregnancy we spent many evenings sitting side by side watching television, my husband's hand on my stomach, waiting for the next movement. With the second pregnancy we weren't able to relax together as much and we missed that special sharing time.

> *Often in the night when our baby was moving,*
> *I would reach for my husband's hand*
> *and place it on my stomach*
> *so he could share the joy with me.*

The first time my husband ever felt life, we were just resting with his head on my abdomen, talking about the baby and he felt it! I think that was really special to him. To be honest, I was disappointed he didn't spend the entire pregnancy with his hand on my belly waiting for movement—or at least a little more of it.

• • •

The baby would be moving and kicking
and my husband would put his hand on my stomach.
Without fail, the baby would stop. We laughed
about it a lot.

• • •

I always loved the
stomach pats and rubs Ray gave me
to say good night to the baby
while we lay in bed.

Our baby is a hard kicker, especially from 10-11 P.M. My husband can sometimes calm him by putting his hand on him.

> *My husband told me one night*
> *with his hand on my tummy*
> *that he gave the baby over to God.*
> *That was comforting.*
> *We're not alone in our journey.*

I know that my husband prayed for our baby and me every morning on the way to work. That encouraged me.

*M*others *S*peak
TALKING TO MY BABY

One night my husband leaned toward my stomach with a cardboard tube against his mouth like a megaphone, and talked to our baby through it.

**Randy would get right down
next to my stomach and talk to our baby
in detail, telling him
how they'd go fishing together.**

When our baby's due date arrived, my husband put his face to my navel and called loudly, "It's O.K. You can come out now!"

SIBLINGS AND THE PREBORN

Stork and cabbage-patch stories have disappeared from most parental explanations of new babies. Many parents tell siblings about their preborn brother or sister long before birth.

That early knowledge can provoke early sibling rivalry. In *Raising Brothers and Sisters Without Raising the Roof*, one family reported that their child approached his mother's protruding abdomen, pressed his nose against it and ordered, "Come out and fight!"

Another family reported this exchange:

Mom: I hope it's a boy.
Dad: I'd like a girl.
Child: I hope it isn't anything!

Despite this risk of rivalry, it's wise to tell children of the baby before birth. In *The Pregnancy Experience,* Dr. Elizabeth Whelan advises parents not to wait to tell their children. One mother commented to her, "Almost from the beginning they hear you discussing it and then there's always some clod on the elevator who says to the child, 'Say, I hear you're going to have a baby brother pretty soon.'"

You're wise to tell them, before someone else does.

When they know, rivalry isn't the only feeling that emerges. Excitement, anticipation, and love for their new brother or sister also blossom.

They become curious about the baby's appearance and size. They thrill to his kicks. Some siblings enjoy going along to the doctor's office and listening to the baby's heartbeat. Other moms tape-record the heartbeat sounds and play the recording for the family.

*M*others *S*peak
SIBLING RIVALRY

Mike and I were saying today how he loves Rachel and Rachel loves him, and he loves Mommy and Mommy loves him—around the circle.

I asked him, "Do you love the baby?"

He thought and said, "Later." He needed time to adjust and he knew it.

> **Sometimes Sally climbs on my lap, pretends to take the baby out and hold it—then she drops him.**

• • • • •

We prayed for the baby and instead of his usual echo, "Yes, Lord," our son said, "No, Lord."

Now he's come full circle. When we pray for the baby now, he says, "Yes, Lord."

*M*others *S*peak

SIBLING LOVE

Sarah's been so lovely. She comes and says, "I love our new baby" and hugs and kisses my tummy. I like to have her feel the feet kick. Whenever she counts the members of our family, she always includes the baby.

> I took the tape recorder to the doctor to record our baby's heartbeat. My daughters provided the introduction on the tape, telling his size, what he was able to do, and added in chorus, "We love our baby!"

The children kiss the baby after bedtime devotions,
but our son Mike kind of giggles at not being able to see her.
My belly button helps, as if we are able to
talk to her through that.

• • • • •

Today my son Mark rubbed
my stomach softly, looked up at me and said,
"I love our baby, Mom."

*M*others *S*peak
INCLUDING SIBLINGS

Our 2½ year old went to the doctor's office with me. She loved using the fetal monitor to hear my baby and helped measure my abdomen. She weighed when I weighed.

We read a lot about fetal development. When we looked at prenatal pictures, I told the kids, "That's what our baby looks like."

• • •

To Sara the baby is a she. She definitely wants a baby sister. I try to prepare her by telling her it might be a boy, and she says that it might be a girl, and we both say, "We'll see what God gives us."

> I read often to our 2½ year old.
> It is usually his idea to read a book
> to the baby.

On walks with a pregnant friend, my children and I sang the ditty, "Two's company, three's a crowd, four on the sidewalk is not allowed." Then we'd laugh because we could fit 6. We counted the 2 preborn babies.

> *My son would say good-bye to the baby each day when he went to school. He also wanted to know how big the baby was. We went to see a prenatal display at the Science Center.*

*My kids were so open about feeling the baby move
that they sometimes embarrassed their friends
by insisting they feel the baby, too.
They helped with planning and shopping.
They dissolved my fourth pregnancy fears!*

Laura gives me rattles for the baby to play with. Today she patted my tummy and said enthusiastically, "Your tummy's getting bigger, Mom!"

*When I told Jodi babies can hear,
she tried yelling
through my belly button.*

One evening in my eighth month, Megan's feet were kicking my jeans' waistband. My son, Matt, came over and lightly tickled them. She pulled her feet back and started kicking in another place. He was thrilled.

• • • • • • •

**I set a plate on my belly at dinner,
and we all watched Audrey
kick it off!**

Resources to Share with Older Children Before the Baby Arrives

☐ *The Wonderful Way that Babies Are Made* by Larry Christenson (Minneapolis, Minn.: Bethany House Publishers, 1982). Illustrated with watercolor paintings, this book tells about human sexuality and prenatal growth as part of God's creation. It's designed in large print for children 3-8 and an optional more detailed smaller print for children 9-14.

☐ *Something Beautiful from God* by Susan Schaeffer Macaulay (Westchester, Ill.: Crossway Books, 1980). In this book, Susan Schaeffer Macaulay tells children about their beginnings and prenatal development—all under the umbrella of God's love. Later chapters deal with children who have special needs. It's illustrated with color and black-and-white photographs and designed for ages 5 and older.

☐ *Getting Ready for Our New Baby* by William Coleman (Minneapolis, Minn.: Bethany House, 1984). Fifty-two free verse devotional readings for children 3-7. The readings help prepare children for adjustments to be made.

☐ *Before You Were Born* by Margaret Sheffield (New York: Alfred A. Knopf, 1984). For children 2-5, *Before You Were Born* describes preborn life with simple words and stylized color illustrations.

☐ *Being Born* by Sheila Kitzinger (New York: Grosset and Dunlap, 1986). Illustrated by Lennart Nillson's detailed and vivid color photographs, *Being Born* describes preborn life for children 3 and older. Includes pictures of birth.

☐ *Prenatal Model.* An actual-size, plastic model of an 11-12-week old preborn baby is available from: Project "Young One," 2125 W. Lawn Ave., Racine, WI 53405. Payment of $1.50 must accompany your order.

11
Sharing with Grandparents and Friends

SHARING WITH GRANDPARENTS AND FRIENDS

A Japanese proverb says, "To understand parents' love, you must have a child of your own."

Sometimes a pregnancy creates a special bond with your parents. Your child is their grandchild; you feel a parent's love; they feel a grandparent's.

Sharing your baby with them—and with other relatives—brings your child into the bonds of your extended family.

When people ask how you are feeling, you can tell them about your nausea and weight gain. You can also tell them about your baby, about his activity or current development:

> *"His heart has started beating already!"*
>
> *"She has fingernails now."*
>
> *"He probably weighs a pound now and is 12 inches long."*
>
> *"He's very active, especially at seven in the evening."*

Sharing information about your baby helps others to realize more concretely his or her existence. It helps them focus on your baby, as well as your pregnancy.

Preborns can also be included in family ritual occasions—the giving and receiving of gifts and cards. Including them in family ritual acknowledges that they are part of the clan. Giving a small Christmas gift to a preborn baby can help siblings begin to accept their new brother or sister.

Mothers Speak
ON FAMILY RITUALS

Our parents bought him Christmas gifts labeled "Baby Whitman." I thought it was neat.

• • • • •

Our baby, Joshua-or-Bridget, gave gifts to "Grandpa and Grandma." He also sent Christmas and Valentine cards to them.

Family Ties

"How are you feeling?"
she asks.
"Tired," I say,
"Baby's growing well, though."

She nods.

She was tired, too,
carrying me.

She hugs me,
and we bond
in silence.

I've joined her side
of motherhood,
both in weary waves of nausea,
and fierce, protective love,

as she once joined
her mother
when she carried me.

Across time and space
my baby links me
with the holy order
of maternity.

CVK

Mothers Speak
ON GRANDPARENTS

We shared the news of our baby when my parents came for Thanksgiving. I wanted to talk about it. My dad was embarrassed and changed the subject. He asked Larry, "Have you been busy lately?" Larry and I dissolved into laughter. "Busy doing what?" Larry asked.

> We told both sets of parents at a Mother's Day dinner in our home. We simply showed them their grandchild's recent ultrasound pictures.

My husband was unable to go with me for the ultrasound, so I took my mom. She had tears in her eyes as she watched her first grandchild and thought of her own seven pregnancies.

• • • • •

There was a change in my relationship with my mother. It was more adult to adult. She shared things she never had before, even things like, "You know, I never liked Aunt Maggie!"

• • • • •

**We videotaped our ultrasound
and let our parents watch it.
They loved it.**

*M*others *S*peak

SHARING WITH THE FAMILY OF GOD

My first-grade students enjoy touching my tummy and talking to the baby. They hug me softly and ask if I feel the baby moving. One kissed my tummy at the end of the school day.

With my first pregnancy, my sister was due to have a baby the same time I was. It was fun to have someone so close to share the experience with. In fact, when I was pregnant the second time I felt kind of lonely, since no one close to me was going through what I was.

I enjoyed my friend's asking,
"Would the two of you like some lunch?" or
"How are the two of you today?"
I liked her easy acceptance.

12
Naming Your Baby

She will give birth to a son,
and you are to give him the name Jesus,
because he will save his people from their sins.
Matthew 1:21

Traditionally parents announce their baby's name at birth. As part of the excitement of announcing a baby's birth, they tell her sex, weight, length, birth time—and name.

But there are alternatives. Some parents create a hyphenated boy-or-girl name, such as Jennie-or-Mike, for their preborn. If ultrasound reveals their child's sex, half of the hyphenated name can be dropped. (Ultrasound technicians are not 100% accurate in observing the baby's sex, however.) Other parents create a prebirth nickname, or use Baby as a proper noun.

Naming your baby before birth is one way to acknowledge his or her humanness before birth.

It does have drawbacks, however. When parents name their child Kathy, only to have him born a boy although the ultrasound technician declared him a girl, they may experience a sense of loss: the baby is not the sex they envisioned. Relatives and friends feel more free to criticize a name announced before birth; they may lobby for a change or diminish the pleasure you feel toward the name you've chosen.

Whatever your timing, it's important to invest thought in your selection. Your baby is important, and his name will last his lifetime.

*M*others *S*peak
NAMING YOUR BABY EARLY

Sara was named already when we were just dating. "If we ever have a daughter, we will name her Sara," we decided. We celebrated the beginning of my pregnancy with her at a restaurant named Sister Sarah's.

> *Before birth we called our baby Jehu because he moved so much.*

We named our baby in the first trimester. It made the pregnancy seem real and the baby a part of our family.

We felt a need to tell people the names we'd chosen.

> *We call our baby BK, for Baby Kitzman.*

When I started wearing maternity clothes, a curious second-grader asked my baby's name. "Matt or Laura," I told him. I hadn't planned on telling people before birth, but after that moment telling others felt right. Our baby had a name!

• • • • •

Our first response to each pregnancy was to name the child. We told people right away, but that was intimidating. People feel free to tell you they don't like a name before a baby is born, but not after. Nevertheless, I feel that preborns are people and should have a name.

*M*others *S*peak
THE FLIP SIDE OF NAMING

When we told the family our name choice, they tried to change our minds. That took the fun out of it.

> We called our baby Russ through pregnancy. We were shocked when we had a girl. I wouldn't do it again.

My husband's family likes to be secretive about names, so we didn't tell them before our baby was born.

**I wanted to keep the names a secret.
I just thought that was part of the surprise
of having a baby.**

HE, SHE, OR IT?

One father says, "It just doesn't seem right to refer to our baby as it."

He has a point. English uses "it" only for objects. People, of course, have gender.

An alternative is to use "he or she" each time you refer to your baby. Another alternative is to use "he" and "she" separately, sometimes choosing one, and sometimes another, until you learn your baby's gender. Experiment—and you'll find what is most comfortable for you.

ONE PLUS TWO MAKES THREE

A nineteenth-century German mathematician, Peter Dirichlet, strongly opposed writing letters. In their lifetimes, many of his friends received no written message from him. But he broke his "no writing" rule with the birth of his first child. He wired his father-in-law: "2+1=3."

Occasionally, when a couple's second child is preborn, friends jokingly refer to their offspring total as "one-and-a-half children." But their math is dead wrong! The day the baby is conceived, she is already 100% human, not just a partial child.

You can acknowledge your preborn child's humanity in your conversation. When people ask, "How many children do you have?" you can answer, "Counting this baby, I have two." Or you can say, "Besides this baby I have one other child." If your preborn is your first, you can answer, "This is our first child." (Actually, the question would be more clearly phrased, "How many other children do you have?"—but we can only control our own language, not that of others.)

Talking about your preborn as your *child* will help make your family, friends, and others more aware of the miracle within your womb. It can be your way of sharing the beauty of life—and God's creation.

13
Postscript for the Postborn

When a child is born, the Chinese say he is 1 year old. On the first anniversary of his birth, he turns 2. In their language, the Chinese acknowledge the continuity of life before and after birth.

We can't expect to change our Western style of counting age, but we may be able to make some minor changes in talking about birth.

Sometimes we say "Baby's arrived" or "Baby's here," describing birth. But, really, baby's been here all along; she's just become more visible. Our change-of-place language is half-accurate. Your baby has journeyed down the birth canal—a 6-8-inch journey—the longest 8 inches he will ever have to travel!

However, it's really more accurate to use change-of-state language: "Our baby has made her appearance," or, "Now we can see our baby." Or we can simply echo the words describing the Birth that gives meaning to all birth: "Unto us a child is born."

Birth

One final push
and you burst forth
wet and wailing,
your farewell to womb
and your hello to world.

Love's labor done
I gaze,
awed to silence.

Your exit and grand entrance
cry for drum rolls
and angel choirs.

Nine months you've
kicked and squirmed,
seen through my womb darkly.

Now face to face
I murmur mother sounds
and touch your cheek and chin.

Love, which bubbled underground
for forty weeks,
bursts skyward in a geyser
and melts heaven's gates.

In one eternal moment
I hear angel choirs
echo my alleluia
to your maker
and mine.

CVK

A **M***other* **S***peaks*

GRAND ENTRANCE

Birth is so significant and earth shattering, it feels as if the world should stop briefly to commemorate it. . . . Afterwards, I just kept saying, "I can't believe it's over." But there was that little girl lying near my heart. And the world did stop for just a little while.

Sheralyn, mother of 3

> . . . no more their wonted joys afford
> The fringed placenta and the knotted cord.
> **Oliver Wendell Holmes**

For there is no king had any other first beginning
For all men have one entrance into life.
The Wisdom of Solomon in the Apocrypha

> A woman giving birth to a child has pain because her time has come; but when her baby is born she forgets the anguish because of her joy that a child is born into the world.
> *John 16:21*

A newborn is merely a small, noisy object, slightly fuzzy at one end, with no distinguishing marks to speak of except a mouth . . . but to its immediate family it is without question the most phenomenal, the most astonishing, the most absolutely unparalleled thing that has yet occurred in the entire history of this planet.
Irving Cobb

> While they were there, the time came for the baby to be born, and she gave birth to her firstborn, a son. She wrapped him in cloths and placed him in a manger, because there was no room for them in the inn. *Luke 2:6-7*

BIRTH: A BABY'S VIEW

For you birth may be exciting, exhausting, dramatic, and painful. You will know your feelings at birth: you'll experience them.

But what does a baby experience? With each contraction of your womb muscles, his curled body straightens. Straightened, his trunk is too long for your womb, and his head presses against your cervix (the opening at the bottom of your uterus).

At first your contractions are gentle pushes which simply interrupt his sleep. But his position is increasingly restricted as your womb thins and lengthens, forcing him to straighten more. He may lose his fluid environment.

As he is pushed through the narrow birth canal he feels pressure. Suddenly, all pressure is released and he enters a strangely huge and brilliant world.

Does he remember his birth? We can't be sure, but if you tried later to force something tight over his head he would fight—wiggling, flinging out his arms, and crying. Such a reaction might be triggered by fleeting memories of birth.

STRANGE, NEW WORLD

After birth your baby may be tired, sore, and a little scared. She wails to protest the whole process. She's bombarded by new sensations from a strange world. How is this new world different for your baby?

☐ The temperature is colder than she's ever experienced. Inside you she's been at a toasty 98.6 degrees, 20 degrees warmer than she is likely to feel in the delivery room.

☐ She feels gravity for the first time. Until now she's been weightless, floating effortlessly.

☐ The light, although she has seen dim glimmerings in your womb, is blinding. She's never experienced anything so bright.

☐ Around her she feels air instead of fluid.

Is it any wonder that she objects to the whole business?

When she settles down, however, she often settles in the same position she favored in the womb—especially if unhampered by clothing and blankets.

Many babies seem alert the first hour after birth, and then sleep for 2-4 hours.

All babies look like me—
bald, wrinkled, and frequently purple
with a bad temper.
Winston Churchill

There is only one pretty child in the world,
and every mother has it.
J.C. Bridge

• • • • • • •

As he [a thirteen-year-old neighbor] peered in the crib, he sucked in his breath through his teeth. "Wow! Sure looks funny, doesn't he? Red and wrinkled like an old man. Hey, you!" he said and thrust a grubby finger into the fist of my *antiseptic* baby. "This new baby sure isn't very good-looking, is he?" he asked cheerfully, blowing his bubble gum into a huge circle.

Mildred Tengboom
Devotions for a New Mother

BEAUTIFUL BABY?

Don't be surprised if your newborn is not a handsome picture-book baby, alert and smiling. He may be covered by vernix—a white, greasy coating that protected his skin from his water environment—or still have some remnants of lanugo (prenatal body hair) on his back and shoulders. His head may be elongated from the pressures of the birth canal. His legs and feet may be bowed from crowding in your womb.

But you will probably think he is absolutely wonderful. And you will be right!

MEASURE FOR MEASURE

Your baby will probably weigh between 5 and 10 pounds. She will probably be 18-23 inches long. Her head circumference will be 12½-14 inches. Average babies weigh 7-7½ pounds, are 20-21 inches long, and have head circumferences of 13½ inches.

> *Definition of a baby:*
> That which makes the home happier, love stronger, patience greater, hands busier, nights longer, days shorter, purses lighter, clothes shabbier, the past forgotten, the future brighter.
> **Marion Lawrence**

THE SIGHT OF YOUR FACE

A newborn is nearsighted; he can focus only on objects 8-12 inches from him. He notices sharp dark-light contrasts and is interested in a black-and-white bull's eye pattern or diagonal black-and-white stripes. A newborn's interest is drawn to the edges of a pattern or object, rather than its interior. Don't be surprised if your baby may at times prefer studying your hairline to looking into your eyes.

Newborns seem to have a special liking for faces. In one study babies who had never seen a human face chose to look at a picture of a normal face over a picture of a face that had the features scrambled. He may follow your face with his eyes if you move it slowly from side to side.

While it takes God
only nine months to make a baby . . .
it takes a lifetime to make a parent!
Helen Good Brenneman
Meditations for the Expectant Mother

AT HOME WITH NOISE

You don't need to whisper to make your baby comfortable. She's been hearing your noisy interior for several months. She likes rhythmic noises, perhaps because they remind her of your constant heartbeat that dominated her life before birth.

However, she will startle at a sudden, loud noise. She will thrust her arms out and up, and then pull them back close to her chest. She may cry.

Newborns find soft music pleasing, and they prefer music to noise. They like vocal music over instrumental, and they prefer human voices to other sounds. Many babies seem to prefer higher-pitched women's voices to those of men. Often a baby will choose her mother's voice over the voice of another woman. And babies can tell the differences between sounds. They react more to normal rhythmic speech than to nonsense vowels.

In one study when newborns were shown pictures of faces making "ah" and "ee" sounds, they turned their eyes toward the face whose mouth was shaped for the correct phoneme. In another study, newborns could tell the differences in phonemes (the smallest distinguishable units of sound). When researchers played a voice repeating a sound, babies sucked harder and their hearts beat faster. But eventually they grew bored with it, and their sucking and heart rates slowed. When the sound changed to a new sound the babies heard the difference and again sucked faster. Babies heard such small changes as the change from "pa" to "ba."

A MATTER OF TASTE

At birth, newborns show they prefer the scent of bananas and vanilla over the smell of rotten eggs and shrimp. They turn their heads away from strong odors.

Babies of less than a week will consistently turn their head toward their mother's breast pad and away from another woman's breast pad, recognizing the scent of their mother's milk without her presence.

They can also taste. Babies as young as twelve hours will gurgle their satisfaction at a drop of sugar-water and grimace at a drop of lemon juice.

NEWBORN MIMES

Swiss psychologist Jean Piaget first studied babies' imitations of adult facial movements. He concluded that the earliest imitations begin at 8-12 months. In 1973 Olga Maratos, a doctoral student testing 7-week-olds, told him of her studies.

"Do you remember what I am doing?" she said. "I am sticking out my tongue at the babies, and do you know what they are doing?"

"You may tell me," Piaget replied.

"They are sticking out their tongues right back at me! What do you think of that?"

Piaget puffed his pipe and thought a moment about her challenge to his theory.

"I think that's very rude," he replied.

Four years later, in 1977, Andrew Meltzoff and M. Keith Moore demonstrated that babies only twelve days old could imitate an adult sticking out his tongue.

In 1981 they used still younger babies. "We had 1 baby 42 minutes old . . . " said Meltzoff. "We washed it and tested it. We found that even newborns could imitate adults."

Babies imitate not only by sticking out their tongues, but also by opening their mouths into a large circle, and by puckering and protruding their lips.

Mothers Speak
A BACKWARD GLANCE

I got so used to a little foot inside, over on the left,
that I sometimes miss it today.

•   •   •   •   •

After delivery, not having the baby move anymore was sometimes a
letdown—a boring stomach again. . . . But it was worth it to see our baby
and hold him. We were amazed at what was so perfectly formed in the
womb. Now we could see and love and care for him. The love for our
newborn was indescribable. We would give our lives for our baby.

LOOKING AHEAD

A child more than all other gifts
That earth can offer to declining man
Brings hope with it, and forward-looking thoughts.
William Wordsworth

As your baby grew in your womb, you dreamed what he would be like—curly or straight hair, blue or brown eyes, his personality shy or vivacious.

Children are gifts from God; and we, as parents, are granted an awesome—and wonderful—responsibility to nurture them for 18-plus years.

Now that your baby is born, you have reached the exciting second stage of your child's life. As your baby grows and develops outside your womb, you and your child will discover together, love together, laugh and play together. You have much to look forward to. What an adventure this parenting business is!

> Oh, cleaning and scrubbing will wait for tomorrow,
> But children grow up, as I've learned to my sorrow,
> So quiet down, cobwebs. Dust, go to sleep,
> I'm rocking my baby. Babies don't keep.
> **Ruth Hulburt Hamilton**
> **"Song for a Fifth Child"**

Resources

Special thanks to three women from Iowa Lutheran Hospital—Molly Yap of Library Services, Sandy Huisman, R.D., Assistant Director of Nutrition Services, and Lynn Koch, R.D., Clinical Dietitian—and to the mothers who shared their pregnancy journeys and journals with us.

Barclay, Lisa. *Infant Development*. New York: Holt, Rinehart and Winston, 1985.

Brenneman, Helen Good. *Meditations for the Expectant Mother*. Scottdale, Penn.: Herald Press, 1968, 1985.

Brewer, Gail, and Janice Greene. *Right from the Start*. Emmaus, Penn.: Rodale Press, 1981.

Brown, Judith. *Nutrition for Your Pregnancy*. Minneapolis: University of Minnesota Press, 1983.

Brown, Laverne. *The Year of Birth*. Paducah, Ky.: Lake Press, 1988.

Burrow, G., and T. Ferris. *Medical Complications During Pregnancy*. Philadelphia: W.B. Saunders Company, 1988.

Calladine, Carole, and Andrew Calladine. *Raising Brothers and Sisters without Raising the Roof*. New York: Harper and Row, 1983.

Caveney, Sylvia. *Inside Mom*. New York: St. Martin's Press, 1976.

Chesler, Phyllis. *With Child: A Diary of Motherhood*. New York: Thomas Crowel, 1979.

Christenson, Larry. *The Wonderful Way That Babies Are Made*. Minneapolis: Bethany House, 1982.

Coleman, William. *Getting Ready for Our New Baby*. Minneapolis: Bethany House, 1984.

Day, Beth, and Margaret Liley. *The Secret World of a Baby*. New York: Random House, 1968.

Darragh, Colleen. *The Pregnancy Day-by-Day Book*. New York: Harper & Row/Madison Press, 1983.

Davis, John. *The Christian's Guide to Pregnancy and Childbirth*. Westchester, Ill.: Crossway Books, 1986.

Eisenberg, Arlene. *What to Expect When You're Expecting*. New York: Workman Publishing, 1984.

Evans, Debra. *The Complete Book on Childbirth*. Wheaton, Ill.: Tyndale, 1986.

Fanaroff, Avory, and Richard Martin. *Neonatal-Perinatal Medicine: Diseases of Fetus and Infant*. St. Louis, Mo.: C.V. Mosby Company, 1983.

Fenlon, Arlene, Ellen McPherson, and Lovell Dorchak. *Getting Ready for Childbirth*. Englewood Cliffs, N.J.: Prentice-Hall, Inc., 1979.

Flanagan, Geraldine. *The First Nine Months of Life*. New York: Simon and Schuster, 1965.

Haley, Alex. *Roots*. Garden City, NY: Doubleday and Company, Inc., 1976.

Halpern, Seymour. *Quick Reference to Clinical Nutrition*, second edition. Philadelphia: J.B. Lippincott Company, 1987.

Heiman, Carrie J. *The Nine-Month Miracle*. Liguori, Mo.: Ligouri Publications, 1986.

Heinowitz, Jack. *Pregnant Fathers*. Englewood Cliffs, N.J.: Prentice-Hall, 1982.

Houtman, H., ed. *Six Days*. Toronto: Wedge Publishing Foundation, 1971.

Klaus, Marshal, and John Kennell. *Maternal-Infant Bonding*. St. Louis, Mo.: C.V. Mosby Company, 1976.

Langman, Jan. *Medical Embryology*, third edition. Baltimore: Williams and Wilkins Company, 1975.

LeJeune, Jerome, and Albert Liley. *The Tiniest Humans*. Santa Ana, Calif.: Robert L. Sassone, 1977.

Luddington-Hoe, Susan. *How to Have a Smarter Baby*. New York: Bantam Books, 1985.

Lutheran Church of America, *Occasional Services: A Companion to Lutheran Book of Worship*. Minneapolis: Augsburg Publishing House; Philadelphia: Board of Publication, Lutheran Church in America, 1982.

Macauley, Susan Schaeffer. *Something Beautiful from God*. Westchester, Ill.: Crossway Books, 1980.

Maurer, Daphne, and Charles Maurer. *The World of the Newborn*. New York: Basic Books, 1988.

Moyle, Peter. *How to Be a Pregnant Father*. Secaucius, N.J.: Lyle Stuart, Inc., 1977.

Nilsson, Lennart, and Mirjam Furuhjelm, et al. *A Child Is Born*. New York: Delacorte Press/Seymour Lawrence, 1977.

Niswander, Keith. *Manual of Obstetrics*, third edition. Boston: Little, Brown, and Company, 1987.

O'Connor, Sarah. *The Nine-Month Journey*. Nashville, Tenn.: Abingdon Press, 1984.

Peck, M. Scott. *The Road Less Traveled*. New York: Simon and Schuster, 1978.

Pennebaker, Ruth, and Libby Wilson. *Stork Realities*. New York: Harper and Row, 1985.

Pernoll, Martin, and Ralph Benson. *Current Obstetric and Gynecologic Diagnosis and Treatment*. Norwalk, Conn.: Appleton and Lange, 1987.

Pritchard, Jack, and Paul MacDonald. *Williams Obstetrics*, 16th edition. New York: Appleton-Century-Crofts, 1980.

Rank, Maureen. *Free to Grieve*. Minneapolis: Bethany House, 1985.

Restak, Richard. *The Infant Mind*. Garden City, N.Y.: Doubleday and Company, 1986.

Shettles, Landrum, and Roberts Rugh. *From Conception to Birth: The Drama of Life's Beginnings*. New York: Harper and Row, 1971.

_____, and David Rorvik. *Rites of Life: The Scientific Evidence for Life Before Birth*. Grand Rapids, Mich.: Zondervan, 1983.

Shils, Maurice. *Modern Nutrition in Health and Disease*, seventh edition. Philadelphia: Lea, Febiger, 1988.

Smith, David. *Mothering Your Unborn Baby*. Philadelphia: W.B. Saunders Company, 1979.

Stern, Ellen Sue. *Expecting Change: The Emotional Journey through Pregnancy*. New York: Simon and Schuster, 1986.

Tengboom, Mildred. *Devotions for a New Mother*. Minneapolis: Bethany House, 1983.

Vaughan, V., R. McKay, and R. Behrman. *Nelson Textbook of Pediatrics*, eleventh edition. Philadelphia: W.B. Saunders Company, 1979.

Verny, Thomas. *The Secret Life of the Unborn Child*. New York: Summit Books, 1981.

Whelan, Elizabeth. *Eating Right: Before, During and After Pregnancy*. Wauwatosa, Wis.: American Baby Books, 1982.

_____. *The Pregnancy Experience*. New York: W.W. Norton, 1978.

Williams, Sue. *Nutrition and Diet Therapy*, sixth edition. St. Louis: Time, Mirrow/Mosby, 1989.

Willke, Jack, and Barbara Willke. *Abortion: Questions and Answers,* Rev. ed. Cincinnati, Ohio: Hayes Publishing Company, 1988.

Wilson, Jane, comp. *In Loving Arms*. Poulsbo, Wash.: Little Balm Books, 1986.

Periodicals

Birnholz, Jason C., and Beryl Benacerraf. "The Development of Human Fetal Hearing" in *Science*, 222 (1983), pp. 516-518.

Cannon, Margaret. "Tapping the Memories of Life in the Womb" in *Macleans*, September 23, 1981, pp. 46-47.

Clapp, Rodney. "Is the Traditional Family Biblical?" *Christianity Today*, September 16, 1988, pp. 24ff.

DeCasper, Anthony, and William Fifer. "Of Human Bonding: Newborns Prefer Their Mothers' Voices" in *Science*, 208 (1980), pp. 1174-1176.

Drife, J.O. "Can the Fetus Listen and Learn?" in *British Journal of Obstetrics and Gynaecology*, 92 (1985), pp. 777-779.

Edelman, Gay. "Babies in Motion" in *Redbook*, October 1983, p. 34.

Fisher, Stanley, and Peter Karl. "Maternal Ethanol Use and Selective Fetal Malnutrition" in *Recent Developments in Alcoholism*, 6 (1988), pp. 277-289.

Fletcher, John, and Mark Evans. "Maternal Bonding in Early Fetal Ultrasound Examinations" in *New England Journal of Medicine,* 308 (1983), pp. 382-393.

Forman, Michael, and Judi Lowenburg Forman. "After a Baby Dies" in *Parents*, August 1988, pp. 114ff.

Friedrich, Otto. "What Do Babies Know?" in *Time*, August 15, 1983, pp. 52-59.

Gagnon, Robert, et al. "Stimulation of Human Fetuses with Sound and Vibration" in *American Journal of Obstetrics and Gynecology*, 155 (1986), pp. 848-851.

Gilinsky, Rhoda. "Bringing Up Baby" in *Publishers Weekly*, June 9, 1989, pp. 20-27.

Grossman, John. "Born Smart" in *Health*, March 1985, pp. 28ff.

Kolata, Gina. "Recollections from the Womb" in *Science*, 84, December 1984, pp. 84-85.

_____. "Studying Learning in the Womb" in *Science*, 225 (1984), pp. 302-303.

Liley, A.W. "The Foetus as a Personality" in *Australian-New Zealand Journal of Psychiatry*, 6 (1972), pp. 99-105.

"Mama, Talk to Your Baby" in *Newsweek*, November 2, 1987, p. 75.

Meltzoff, Andrew, and Keith Moore. "Imitation of Facial and Manual Gestures by Human Neonates" in *Science*, October 1977, pp. 75-78.

Miller, Juli Ann. "Window on the Womb" in *Science News,* February 2, 1985, pp. 75-76.

Nelson, Martha. "Listening in the Womb" in *Omni*, December 1985, p. 24.

Newman, V., R. Lyon, and P. Anderson. "Evaluation of Prenatal Vitamin-Mineral Supplements" in *Clinical Pharmacy*, 6 (1987), pp. 770-727.

Palmer, Jacqueline. "Sensing in the Womb" in *American Biology Teacher*, 49:7 (1987), pp. 411-417.

Powledge, Tabitha. "Windows on the Womb" in *Psychology Today*, May 1983, pp. 36-42.

Roberts, Marjory. "Class Before Birth" in *Psychology Today*, May 1987, p. 41.

Shetler, Donald. "Prenatal Music Experiences" in *Music Educators Journal*, March 1985, pp. 26-27.

Smith, Rachel. "Pregnancy and Childbirth: A Theological Event" in *The Christian Century*, 96 (1979), pp. 1262-1266.

Span, Paula. "Sound Advice" in *Redbook*, March 1984, p. 32.

Stainton, M. Colleen. "The Fetus: A Growing Member of the Family" in *Family Relations*, 34 (1985), pp. 321-326.

Thomson, A.O., and O.E. Pratt. "Alcohol and Brain Damage" in *Human Toxicology*, 7 (1988), pp. 455-463.

Warren, K., and R. Bast. "Alcohol-Related Birth Defects: An Update" in *Public Health Reports*, 103:6 (1988), pp. 638-642.

Waterson, E.J., and I.M. Murray-Lyon. "Drinking and Smoking Patterns Amongst Women Attending an Antenal Clinic before Pregnancy" in *Alcohol and Alcoholism*, 24:2 (1989), pp. 153-162.

Webb, S., M. Hochberg, and M. Sher. "Fetal Alcohol Syndrome: A Report of Case" in *JADA*, 116 (1988), pp. 196-198.

Wein, Bibi. "Tiny Dancers" in *Omni*, May 1988, p. 122.

"What Your Unborn Baby Hears" in *Woman's World*, January 17, 1989, p. 12.

"When Mom Speaks to Baby on This Phone, There's a Pregnant Pause" in *People Weekly*, October 31, 1988, p. 83.

Worthington-Roberts, Bonnie, and Jeannette Endres. "Nutrition Management of Adolescent Pregnancy: A Technical Support Paper" in *Journal of American Dietetic Association*, 89:1 (1989), pp. 105-109.

Wynn, M., and A. Wynn. "Nutrition Around Conception and the Prevention of Low Birthweight" in *Nutritional Health*, 6:1 (1988), pp. 37-52.